LEARN TO Cook

LEARN TO Cook

35 fun and easy recipes

for children aged 7 years +

CICO kidz

This edition published in 2023 by CICO Kidz
An imprint of Ryland Peters & Small Ltd

20–21 Jockey's Fields,   341 E 116th St
London WC1R 4BW   New York NY 10012

www.rylandpeters.com

10 9 8 7 6 5 4 3 2 1

First published in 2014 as *My First Cookbook*

A CIP catalog record for this book is available from the
Library of Congress and the British Library.

ISBN: 978-1-80065-188-3

Printed in China

Editors: Clare Sayer and Susan Akass
Designer: Barbara Zuñiga
Step artworks: Rachel Boulton
Animal artworks: Hannah George

• All spoon measurements are level unless otherwise specified.

• Both US cup sizes or imperial and metric measurements have been given. Use one set of measurements only and not a mixture of both.

• All eggs are US large (UK medium) unless otherwise stated. This book contains recipes made with raw eggs. It is prudent for more vulnerable people, such as pregnant and nursing mothers, babies and young children, invalids and the elderly, to avoid uncooked dishes made with eggs.

• Some of the recipes contain nuts and should not be consumed by anyone with a nut allergy.

• Ovens should be preheated to the specified temperatures. All ovens work slightly differently. We recommend using an oven thermometer and suggest you consult the maker's handbook for any special instructions, particularly if you are cooking in a fan-assisted oven, as you will need to adjust temperatures according to manufacturer's instructions.

Contents

Introduction

We all need food! It gives us energy, it keeps us healthy, it is great to share with other people, and—if you cook it right—it tastes delicious. These are all excellent reasons to learn to cook, but above all, cooking is fun!

This book teaches you to cook by guiding you through every stage of 35 delicious recipes, showing you how to do everything, from breaking an egg to grating a carrot. It is divided into four chapters: Snacks and Light Meals, which has great ideas for exciting snacks, breakfasts, and lunches; Proper Meals, for when you want to cook supper for your family or friends (everyone will be impressed by these); Desserts, because every good meal should end with something sweet; and Party Food, because getting ready for a party is a really good time to have fun cooking.

You must always ask an adult before you start any cooking and, most importantly, whenever the recipe tells you to, because using kitchen equipment can be dangerous. However, the more you cook, the more skills you will learn, and the safer you will become. Each recipe has full instructions, but we have also included a techniques section to help you, whatever you are cooking.

As another way of helping you, we have graded each recipe with a grading of one, two, or three smiley faces—see opposite. Level one recipes are the easiest. In these, there are only a few steps and you do not need to use sharp knives or to cook anything on the stovetop (hob). Level two recipes are a bit more complicated and you will need to cut up ingredients using a sharp knife. For level three, you will need to use a knife and to cook on the stovetop (hob)—it helps if you are a bit taller when cooking these ones!

So, are you ready to get cooking? Choose a recipe and check out what ingredients you need!

Project levels

Level 1
These have only a few stages and require just a little adult help.

Level 2
These include more stages, and some trickier techniques, and require some adult help.

Level 3
These are longer and require adult help for most of the stages.

Useful kitchen equipment

Strainer (sieve)
Colander
Vegetable peeler
Grater
Garlic crusher
Sharp knives
Measuring pitcher (jug)
Weighing scales
Measuring cups
Measuring spoons
Wire whisk
Bamboo skewers
Spatulas
Palette knife
Pastry brush
Rolling pin
Baking sheets
Wire cooling rack
Chopping board
Egg cup
Ovenproof dishes
loaf pan (tin) 8 x 4 x 2 in. (1lb)

Plastic wrap (clingfilm)
Baking parchment
Paper towels (kitchen paper)
Mixing bowls in different sizes
Heatproof glass bowls
Microwave-safe bowls
Saucepans
Skillets (frying pans)
Kitchen timer
Metal cooking tongs
Oven gloves
Lemon squeezer
Trivet
Kitchen scissors
Electric beater (whisk)
Wooden spoon
Vegetable brush

Kitchen safety
-read this before you start cooking!

- Always wash your hands before you start cooking and after touching raw meat.
- Tie long hair back so that it is out of the way.
- Wear an apron to keep your clothes clean.
- Make sure your ingredients are fresh and within their use-by date.
- When using sharp knives, electrical equipment, or the stovetop (hob,) microwave, or oven, always ask an adult to help you.
- Use oven mitts when holding hot pans or dishes.
- Use a chopping board when using a sharp knife or metal cookie cutters—this protects the work surface and will help to stop the knife from slipping.
- Keep your work surface clean and wipe up any spills on the floor so that you don't slip.
- Don't forget to clear up afterward!

Tips and techniques

Using an oven

Many of the recipes in this book use the oven to cook the food. For these recipes the first thing you must do is turn on the oven. This is because the oven needs to be hot enough to cook the food you put into it and it takes a little while to heat up.

- Always ask an adult before using the oven.
- The recipe instructions always tell you at what temperature to set your oven. Ask an adult to show you how to set the oven to the correct temperature.
- On most ovens there is a light, which goes out when the oven reaches the temperature you have set, and then it is ready to use.
- Always use oven mitts when putting food into the oven or taking it out. Even when the dish you put in is cold, you can easily burn yourself on the hot racks or the oven door.
- When you take a hot dish out of the oven, always put it onto a heatproof board or trivet so that you don't burn the work surface.
- Whenever you cook food in the oven, you need to be sure that the food doesn't stick to the oven dish or pan. For cakes and cookies, line the pan with some baking parchment. (To do this, stand the pan on the parchment and draw around it to get the correct size paper. Cut out the shape of the pan and put it in the pan)
- For other types of recipes, prepare your dish by greasing it—put a little oil or butter on some kitchen paper and rub it all over the pan.

Using the stovetop (hob)

You must always have an adult with you when using the stovetop.

- If you are not tall enough to work safely at the stovetop, you must use a small step to stand on, with an adult helping you.
- When using the stovetop, make sure that saucepan handles don't stick out over the front of the stovetop where you could knock into them and knock off the pan.
- Don't have the heat too high—it is easy to burn your food.
- When using a skillet (frying pan) use a spatula to move the food around so that the pieces don't stick and burn.
- When a pan of water begins to boil, turn down the heat so it doesn't spill all over the stovetop.
- Always remember to turn off the heat when you've finished cooking.
- When you take a pan off the stovetop, always put it onto a heatproof board or trivet so that you don't burn the work surface.

Weighing and measuring

When you are cooking you will often have to weigh or measure ingredients. For baking recipes (such as making a cake,) you need to be very accurate or they won't work, but for most cooking, exact measurements are not so important. For instance, if you prefer to have more spice in your soup, that is up to you! However, it is better to start with the measurements given in a recipe when you first try it and then, if you want to, you can change it next time.

This book uses two different types of measurements: one for children in the USA, and one for children in the UK. Follow one type of measurement all the way through a recipe and don't swap between the two—use either all the first measurements given (USA style) or all the second ones, which are in brackets, (UK style.) You will need measuring cups or weighing scales for large quantities, measuring spoons for small quantities and measuring cups or a pitcher (jug) for liquids.

Using a microwave

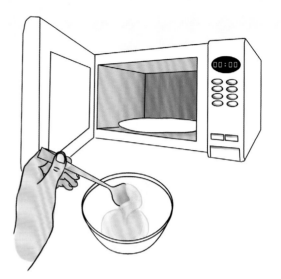

Using a microwave is a quick and easy way to heat and melt ingredients, but you must be careful and always ask an adult before using one. You should also follow these safety tips.

- Always use microwave-safe bowls and never put anything made of metal into the microwave.
- When heating anything in the microwave, you must take great care to stir the heated ingredient thoroughly before using or eating it—even if it seems lukewarm on the outside, it could be burning hot inside. When you stir melted chocolate or jelly (jam,) for example, you will spread the heat evenly and avoid these hot spots. Heat on a medium or low setting for short lengths of time, rather than continuously, and keep checking at least every 30 seconds.
- Microwave ovens are all different, so timings for your microwave may be different from the ones given in the recipe

Melting chocolate

- Break the chocolate into a microwave-safe bowl.
- Ask an adult to help you heat it on low for 30 seconds, then stir it, and then heat it again for another 30 seconds. Keep checking, heating for 30 seconds and stirring until the chocolate is nearly melted with just a few lumps left.
- Remove the bowl from the microwave and stir it until it is smooth. Take care that the chocolate doesn't overheat.
- Use oven mitts to take the hot bowl out of the microwave.

Washing fruit and vegetables

Before you use fruit and vegetables you should always wash them to clean off any dirt or chemical sprays. Put them into a colander in the sink and wash them under the cold faucet (tap.) You may have to use a vegetable brush to scrub the soil off root vegetables, such as potatoes and carrots.

Using knives

Good cooks must learn to use knives properly, and you should ask an adult to teach you. If you use it properly, a sharp knife is safer than a blunt one, because it won't slip, but you must hold the food firmly, and keep your fingers out if the way. Always use a chopping board and one of the following three techniques:

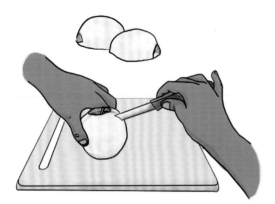

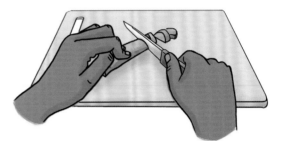

The "Claw" cutting technique

The "Claw" cutting technique is used for chopping or slicing foods, such as carrots or onions, into smaller pieces:

- Cut the food in half (using the bridge cutting technique) so that you have a flat side. Place the flat side of the food down on the chopping board so that it is steady.
- Shape the fingers of one hand into a claw shape, tucking the thumb inside the fingers. Rest the claw on the food to be sliced to hold it firm.
- Holding the knife in the other hand, slice the food, making sure to move the "clawed" fingers back as the knife slices closer.

The "Bridge" cutting technique

The "Bridge" cutting technique is used for cutting larger things (for example apples, tomatoes, or onions) into smaller pieces:

- Hold the food by forming a bridge with your thumb on one side of the food and your index finger on the other side. Hold the knife in your other hand with the blade facing down, guide the knife under the bridge, and cut through the food.
- For some soft items, such as tomatoes, it might be easier to puncture the tomato skin with the point of the knife before cutting.

Chopping herbs

- Put the pile of herbs on a board. Have the flat of one hand on top of the knife and the other on the handle and rock the knife over the herbs.
- Another way of cutting up herbs is to put them in a small cup and snip them with scissors.

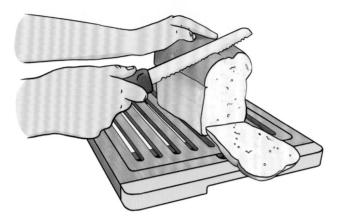

Cutting bread

Ready-sliced bread is easy to use but the tastiest bread usually needs slicing. Use a serrated bread knife.

- Put the loaf of bread on a bread board.
- Hold the bread with one hand flat on the top and your thumb tucked out of the way. Decide how thick you want your slice to be—don't try and cut it too thin.
- Start to cut, using the bread knife like a saw and going smoothly backwards and forwards.
- Keep checking that you are cutting straight— this needs lots of practice.

Peeling

To peel carrots (or other vegetables, such as zucchini/courgettes or cucumbers):

- Trim off the ends.
- Hold the carrot at one end and rest the other end on a chopping board.
- Starting halfway along it, run the vegetable peeler down the carrot towards the board and away from your hand.
- Turn the carrot a little and peel the next strip in the same way. Keep turning and peeling until all of one end has been peeled.
- Turn the carrot up the other way, and hold the other end while you peel the second half.

To peel fruit, like apples, or kiwi fruit:

- Rest the apple in the palm of your hand. Starting at the top, run the vegetable peeler around the apple, turning it as you go so that you create a spiral of peel.
- Keep turning the apple as you peel—see how long a strip you can make!

Grating

Cooks grate all sorts of things—cheese, chocolate, carrots, zucchini (courgettes)—to make them small so they will mix into a recipe or be sprinkled on top. Be careful when grating because it is very easy to grate your fingers!

• Stand the grater on a flat chopping board or plate so that it is firm and doesn't wobble. Hold it firmly on the top.

• Hold the food with your fingertips. Grate from top to bottom keeping your fingers well away from the grater.

• Only grate big pieces of food and don't try to grate right to the end—discard the pieces when they get too small to hold safely.

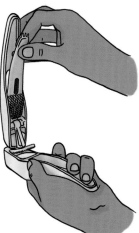

Preparing garlic

Garlic is used in lots of recipes to add flavor. To prepare it:

• Peel off the white papery skin from around the bulb.

• Pull off as many cloves as you need in the recipe. If you really like garlic or if the cloves are very small you can always add more than the recipe says!

• Lightly crush each clove with a rolling pin. This will split the skin and it will come off easily.

• Put the cloves in a garlic press (one or two at a time) and squeeze it hard over the other ingredients until all the juicy garlic comes out of the holes.

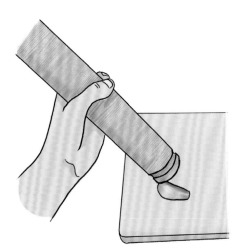

Folding

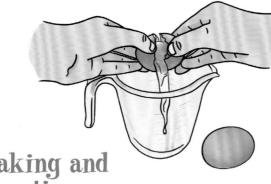

Some recipes ask you to fold in ingredients. Folding is a way of mixing light ingredients into heavier ones without squashing out any air.

- Use a metal rather than a wooden spoon to cut through the mixture in a gentle figure eight, rather than stirring it around and around as you would with a wooden spoon.
- Every so often, scrape around the edge of the bowl to make sure all of the ingredients are mixed together.

Breaking and separating eggs

In some recipes you need the whole egg so you have to break it into a bowl and whisk the white and yolk together with a balloon whisk or fork. Other recipes need either whites or yolks, so you need to learn to separate the two.

- To break an egg, tap it firmly on the side of the bowl to crack it (not too hard or you will smash it completely!) Then put your thumbs into the crack and pull the two halves apart. Scoop out any pieces of shell with another bigger piece of shell.

- To separate the egg white from the yolk, carefully break the egg onto a flat plate, place an egg cup over the yolk and then let the white slide off into a bowl leaving the yolk behind. If you want to beat the whites, make sure that the bowl is very clean and grease-free.

Rolling out pastry dough

- Use plenty of flour on your work surface to stop the pastry sticking to the surface. Put some on your rolling pin too.
- When you roll pastry, push down and away from you.
- Keep moving the pastry, to make sure it hasn't stuck, and add a little more flour if it does stick.
- Try not to handle the pastry too much—it needs to stay cold and your hands will make it hot!

Using boullion (stock)

Instead of just adding water to soups and sauces, cooks add boullion (stock) to give them more flavor. You can make it at home by boiling meat bones, vegetables and water, but lots of people buy it ready-made from the supermarket. You can buy it in cartons and packets (sachets) which are ready to use, or you can buy it in cubes, powders, or jellies which need mixing with boiling water before you use them. For these kinds:

- Read the instructions on the packet carefully.
- Ask an adult to help you boil a kettle and to pour the correct amount of boiling water into a measuring pitcher (jug.)
- Add as many cubes or as much jelly or powder as it says on the packet and stir until it dissolves.

Snacks and Light Meals

Buttermilk pancakes

For a special weekend breakfast, or for the morning after a sleepover, nothing beats a pile of pancakes with crispy bacon and lots of maple syrup. And there is nothing quite so satisfying to make—just watch as the gooey batter turns into golden pancakes before your eyes.

You will need

1¾ cups (225 g) all-purpose (plain) flour

1 tablespoon baking powder

½ teaspoon salt

4 tablespoons superfine (caster) sugar

½ stick (50 g) unsalted butter, plus extra for frying

2 medium eggs, lightly beaten

½ cup (125 ml) milk

½ cup (125 ml) buttermilk

1 teaspoon vanilla extract

maple syrup, to serve

crispy rashers of smoked bacon, to serve (optional)

large heavy skillet (frying pan) (non-stick is easiest)

(makes 16–18)

1 Set a large strainer (sieve) over a large mixing bowl. Tip the flour, baking powder, salt, and sugar into the strainer (sieve) and sift them into the bowl. Make a hole in the center of the mixture.

2 Ask an adult to help you melt the butter in a small saucepan over low heat, or put it in a microwave-proof dish and microwave on MEDIUM for about 20 seconds. Check to see if it has melted, stir and heat again for another 20 seconds. Keep going like this until it has melted.

3 Break the eggs into a pitcher (jug.) To do this tap each one firmly on the side of the bowl to crack it. (Not too hard or you will smash it completely!) Then put your thumbs into the crack and pull the two halves apart. Pick out any pieces of shell using a bigger piece of egg shell as a scoop.

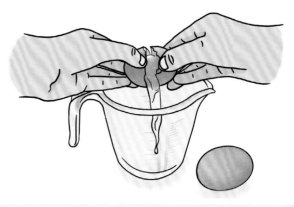

4 Add the milk, buttermilk, melted butter, and vanilla extract to the pitcher (jug) and whisk with a balloon whisk until they are well mixed.

5 Pour the egg mixture into the hole you made in the middle of the flour and then whisk the flour into the liquid. Keep whisking until it's smooth and there are no lumps left.

6 Ask an adult to help you with the next stages of cooking. Put a knob of butter in a large, heavy skillet (frying pan) and ask an adult to help you set it over medium heat. Allow the butter to melt, swirling it so that it coats the bottom of the pan evenly.

buttermilk pancakes **19**

7 To make one pancake, drop 2 or 3 tablespoons of the pancake batter into the hot pan. You will probably be able to fit two or three more pancakes into the pan, but space them out so that they don't run into one another. Cook the pancakes for about 1 minute, or until bubbles start to appear on the surface.

8 Using a spatula, flip the pancakes over and cook the other side until they are golden and well-risen. Remove the pancakes from the pan and keep them warm on a plate covered with aluminum foil. Repeat with the remaining batter.

9 Serve the pancakes with maple syrup and crispy bacon—or with your own favorite topping.

Great on their own, even better with CRISPY BACON!

Herby scrambled eggs

The mark of a good cook is if they can cook eggs perfectly. It's not difficult, but you have to get the timing right, especially if you want your toast to be cooked at the same time. So you need some quick action in this recipe. These herby scrambled eggs are great for lunch, breakfast, or supper.

You will need

small handful of fresh herbs (such as parsley or chives)

2 eggs

salt

4 cherry tomatoes

a slice of bread

unsalted butter

saucepan

(serves 1)

1 Using scissors, snip the herbs into tiny pieces, straight into a mixing bowl.

2 Break the eggs into the bowl. To do this tap each one firmly on the side of the bowl to crack it. (Not too hard or you will smash it completely!) Then put your thumbs into the crack and pull the two halves apart. Pick out any pieces of shell using a bigger piece of shell as a scoop. Add a good pinch of salt and mix with a fork so the yolk breaks up and mixes with the clear part (which is called the white because it goes white when it is cooked.)

3 Remembering to hold your hand in the bridge position (see page 11,) use a small sharp knife to cut each of the tomatoes in half. Put the halves, cut-side down on the board, and cut them into quarters. Add them to the eggs.

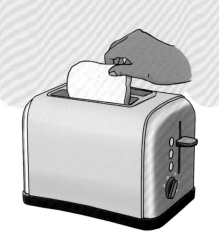

4 Put a slice of bread in the toaster but don't cook it yet. Get the butter out of the fridge.

5 Put a knob of butter in a saucepan and ask an adult to help you melt it over medium (not high) heat. Add the eggs and cook, stirring all the time with a wooden spoon. Keep stirring to break up the egg and to make sure it doesn't stick to the pan.

6 After your eggs have begun to cook, quickly start the toaster, then get back to stirring.

7 When the eggs are almost cooked—so they look only slightly runny—take the pan off the heat and rest it on a pan stand. Keep stirring until the eggs are cooked—the heat from the pan will continue to cook them.

8 Wait for the toast to pop, then put it on a plate, butter it and pile the herby eggs on top.

Butternut squash soup with cheesy croutons ☺ ☺ ☺

This recipe makes a large pot of soup—enough to feed a hungry crowd on a cold winter's day. The butternut squash has a rich sweet flavor and the croutons add a cheesy crunch!

You will need

For the soup:

1 onion

2 carrots

1 medium leek

1 celery stalk

1 tablespoon (15g) unsalted butter

1 tablespoon olive oil

1 butternut squash

1 garlic clove

a 1-in (2.5-cm) piece of root ginger

2 pints (1 litre) vegetable boullion (stock) or boullion (stock) cubes/concentrate

salt and freshly ground black pepper

For the croutons:

6 slices of 1-day-old bread

1 tablespoon olive oil

1 cup (100 g) Cheddar or Parmesan, grated

large saucepan

blender or stick blender

baking sheet

(serves 6–8)

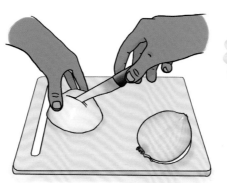

1 Prepare the onion: peel off the papery outside skin and put the onion on a chopping board. Holding your hand in the bridge position (see page 11,) cut the onion in half with a sharp knife. Lay each half flat on the board, trim off any hairy roots, and then cut the onion into small pieces.

2 Use a sharp knife to cut both ends off all the carrots. Remember to cut down on a chopping board. Now peel the carrots with a vegetable peeler like this: hold a carrot at one end and rest the other end on the chopping board. Starting halfway down, run the potato peeler down the carrot, away from your body. Be careful—the peeler is sharp! Turn the carrot to peel the next strip and keep turning and peeling until it is peeled all the way around. Now turn the carrot up the other way and hold the other end while you peel the other half. Now cut them into small pieces.

Tip:

Remember when cutting the carrots, onion, celery, and leek into small pieces keep your hand in the claw position (see page 11.)

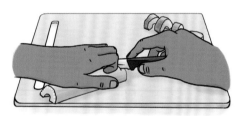

3 Cut off the bottom of the leek where the roots are and cut off any thick, dark leaves at the top. Cut the leek in half along its length and wash it very well under a running cold faucet (tap)—sometimes grit can get caught between the leaves. Chop the leek into small pieces.

4 Trim the ends of the celery and pull off some of the nasty stringy bits from the outside. Chop the celery into small pieces.

5 Put the butter and oil in a large saucepan and ask an adult to help you set it over medium heat. Add the chopped onion, carrots, leek, and celery and cook slowly, stirring every few minutes with a wooden spoon, until they are soft, but not browned. This will take about ten minutes but it won't matter if it cooks for longer while you prepare the butternut squash— you can always turn down the heat to low.

6 While the vegetables are cooking, ask an adult to prepare the butternut squash. **Do not do this yourself** as they are tough and difficult to prepare. If the adult pierces the skin with a sharp knife and then microwaves it on full power for two minutes, this will make it easier to peel and cut. After microwaving they should let it cool for a few minutes, then use a strong vegetable peeler to remove the skin. Next they should stand the squash upright, and cut it in half. Now you can take over again.

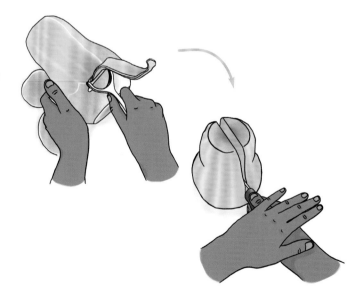

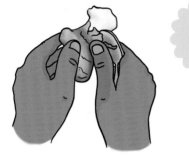

7 Scrape out the seeds with a metal spoon, and then cut the squash into chunks.

8 Peel the papery skin off the garlic clove, and crush the garlic straight into the pan using a garlic crusher.

9 Peel the ginger. The easiest way to do this is with a teaspoon—the skin is very thin so just hold the ginger in one hand and scrape it with the edge of the spoon with the other. Stand the grater on a small plate and grate the ginger. The piece of ginger is quite small so be careful not to grate your fingers. Add it to the pan along with the butternut squash chunks. Give everything a stir, and then continue to cook for 3–4 minutes.

10 Add the boullion (stock.) If you are using boullion (stock) cubes/concentrate ask an adult to help you boil a kettle. Pour 2 pints (1 litre) of water into a pitcher (jug,) add the correct amount of concentrate according to the instructions on the packet and stir until it dissolves, and then pour it into the soup. Season the soup with salt and black pepper. Turn up the heat and bring it to boil, then lower the heat so that it is at a gentle simmer (which means bubbling a little but not boiling.) Continue to cook until the squash is tender. This should take about 20 minutes. Test it by pushing a sharp knife into a piece of squash.

11 Turn off the heat and ask an adult to help you blend the soup until smooth, either in a blender or using a stick blender. Check the seasoning and add more salt or pepper if you think it needs it. If the soup is a little thick, add some extra boullion (stock) or water.

12 Now make the croutons. Ask an adult to turn the oven on to 350°F (180°C) Gas 4.

13 Put the bread flat on the breadboard in a neat pile and use a bread knife to cut off the crusts—remember using a bread knife is like using a saw—you go backward and forward to cut.

14 Cut the bread into squares of about ¾ in (2 cm) and tip into a large bowl. Add the oil and mix with your hands so that the bread is coated in oil. Add the grated cheese and stir well. Tip the croutons out onto a baking sheet. Ask an adult to help you put them into the oven to bake for 15 minutes or until golden and crisp.

15 Reheat the soup gently in a pan over medium heat and then ladle into bowls and scatter some croutons on top.

Add croutons for **CRUNCH**

Carrot soup

A bowl of hot soup is what you really want when it starts getting chillier outside. This tastes really sweet and creamy, but it's very easy because you hardly need any ingredients. Use big carrots, if you can, because you won't have so many to peel!

You will need

....

2 lb 2 oz (1 kg) carrots

1 onion

1 garlic clove (unpeeled)

olive oil, for drizzling

a 14-oz (400-ml) can of coconut milk

400 ml vegetable boullion (stock) or boullion (stock) cubes/concentrate

a small handful of fresh herbs (such as parsley and cilantro/coriander)

heavy-based roasting pan
food processor or blender

(serves 4)

 1 Ask an adult to turn the oven on to 350°F (180°C) Gas 4.

 2 Use a sharp knife to cut both ends off all the carrots. Remember to cut down on a chopping board. Now peel the carrots with a vegetable peeler like this: hold a carrot at one end and rest the other end on the chopping board. 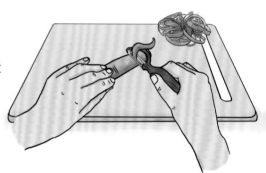 Starting halfway down, run the potato peeler down the carrot, away from your body. Be careful—the peeler is sharp! Turn the carrot to peel the next strip and keep turning and peeling until it is peeled all the way around. Now turn the carrot up the other way and hold the other end while you peel the other half. When you have finished peeling all the carrots, cut them into chunks remembering to keep your hand in the claw position (see page 11.)

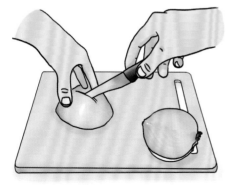 **3** Now prepare the onion: peel off the papery outside skin and put the onion on a chopping board. Holding your hand in the bridge position (see page 11,) cut the onion in half with a sharp knife. Lay each half flat on the board, trim off any hairy roots, and then cut the onion into wedges.

4 Put the onion and carrots into the roasting pan, add the garlic, and drizzle with a little oil. Ask an adult to help you put the pan in the oven and set a timer for fifteen minutes. When it pings, ask an adult to help you take the pan out of the oven and, using a spatula or big spoon, carefully turn the vegetables so that they cook evenly all over. Return them to the oven and set the timer for another fifteen minutes to finish cooking.

Creamy carrot and COCONUT!

5 At the end of the cooking time, ask an adult to help you take the pan out of the oven and carefully spoon the vegetables into a food processor or blender. Squeeze the roasted garlic clove out of its skin and into the processor. You could also use a stick blender for this, (see step 11 on page 26.)

6 Add half the coconut milk, put the lid on the processor and ask an adult to help you run the machine until you have a smooth soup.

7 Pour the puréed soup into a saucepan. Add the rest of the coconut milk and the stock. (If you are using boullion [stock] cubes/concentrate ask an adult to help you boil a kettle. Pour 1¾ cups (400ml) of water into a pitcher (jug,) add the correct amount of concentrate according to the instructions on the packet and stir until it dissolves.)

8 Carefully, using a sharp knife, chop the fresh herbs into very small pieces (see page 11) and then add to the saucepan.

9 Heat the soup gently over a medium heat until it is very hot but not boiling. Taste the soup—but don't burn your mouth—if it is a little too thick, add more stock or water to make it thinner.

Summer salad with crispy croutons

A salad goes well with almost any lunch or supper meal, so it's good to learn how to make one and toss it in dressing. It is even more fun if you have grown the salad leaves and tomatoes yourself, but if you haven't, you will still enjoy making and eating this delicious and healthy salad.

You will need

For the croutons:

4 thick slices of brown or white bread

2 tablespoons olive oil

For the salad:

½ cucumber

about 8 cherry tomatoes (of different colors if you have them)

4 handfuls of baby spinach (or chard) leaves

4 handfuls of arugula (rocket) leaves

2 handfuls of any other salad leaves you'd like to add (such as lollo rosso or batavia)

For the dressing:

1 tablespoon lemon juice

3 tablespoons olive oil

bread knife

roasting pan

glass jar

(serves 4)

1 Start with the croutons: ask an adult to help you turn the oven on to 350°F (180°C) Gas 4.

2 Cut thick slices of bread using a bread knife (see page 11) or use ready-sliced bread. Put each slice of bread flat on the bread board and use the bread knife to cut off the crusts all the way around. Remember that using a bread knife is like using a saw—you go backward and forward to cut. Then cut the slice into fingers about ¾ in (2 cm) wide. Cut the fingers into cubes.

3 Put the cubes into a roasting pan, sprinkle the oil over the top and use your hands to mix the bread around in the oil. Ask an adult to help you put them into the oven and set a timer for 10 minutes.

4 Using oven gloves, take the pan out of the oven and mix the croutons with a wooden spoon. Put back into the oven for 10 more minutes, or until the croutons are golden and crunchy.

5 Meanwhile, to make the salad, slice the cucumber into thin slices using the claw cutting technique (see page 11) and cut the tomatoes in half using the bridge cutting technique (see page 11.)

6 Put the spinach (or chard) and arugula (rocket) in a colander and wash with cold water. Shake gently to get rid of a bit of the water. Put into a big salad bowl with the cucumber and tomatoes, and any other washed salad leaves you'd like to add.

7 Put the lemon juice and olive oil into a glass jar, put the top on tightly and shake it well to mix the dressing. Drizzle the dressing over the salad. Toss everything together with salad serving spoons so that all the leaves are coated with the dressing.

CRUNCHY AND CRISPY—what could be better?

8 Finally, drop in the lovely crispy croutons (add them at the last minute so they don't go soggy in the dressing!) and toss the salad again. Serve immediately.

Little fried mozzarella and tomato sandwiches

These little sandwiches are deliciously hot, crisp and eggy on the outside and gooey and creamy on the inside. They are a popular snack all over Italy. Add slices of ham or a few torn basil leaves on top of the tomatoes if you like.

You will need

16 small, thin slices of bread (use ready-sliced bread)

3–4 tomatoes

6½ oz (185 g) mozzarella cheese

3 eggs

3 tablespoons olive oil, for frying

salt and freshly ground black pepper

bread knife

rectangular shallow dish

nonstick skillet (frying pan)

(serves 4)

1 Put the bread flat on the bread board in a neat pile and use a bread knife to cut off the crusts—remember using a bread knife is like using a saw—you go backwards and forwards to cut.

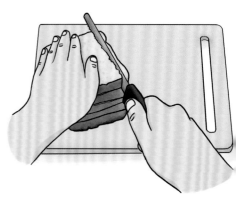

2 Put the tomato on the chopping board and, holding your hand in the bridge position (see page 11) cut it in half with a small sharp knife. Lay the two halves flat on the board and with your hand in the claw position cut them carefully into slices.

3 Make sure the work surface is nice and clean and then lay out eight slices of bread on it. Tear the mozzarella into little pieces and dot it on the bread. Lay the slices of tomato over the top.

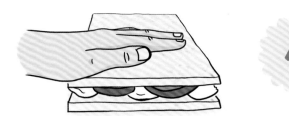

Hot, fried SURPRISES!

4 Top with the remaining bread slices and press them down lightly with the palm of your hand to seal them together.

5 Break the eggs into a bowl. To do this, tap each one firmly on the side of the bowl to crack it. (Not too hard or you will smash it completely!) Then put your thumbs into the crack and pull the two halves apart. Pick out any pieces of shell using a bigger piece of shell as a scoop, then beat with a fork until smooth. Add a pinch of salt and a few turns of pepper to the egg, and then beat them with a fork until they are nice and smooth.

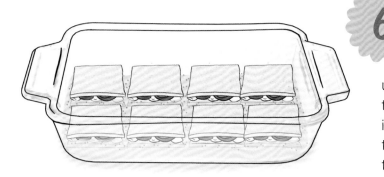

6 Pour the egg mix into a shallow container in which you can fit the sandwiches—an ovenproof dish would be good, or you may have to use two smaller dishes and pour half of the egg into each one. Lay the sandwiches in the egg and leave them for 2–3 minutes to soak it up. Turn them over and leave them for another 2–3 minutes so that the other side is soaked in egg too.

7 Ask an adult to help you heat a little of the olive oil in a nonstick skillet (frying pan) and fry the sandwiches on one side for about 3 minutes, until the bread is golden. You will more than likely have to cook them in at least 2 batches, depending on the size of the pan you have.

8 Ask an adult to help you turn the sandwiches over, using a spatula, and fry them for another 2–3 minutes, until that side is golden too; the cheese inside should be melted.

9 Finally, ask an adult to help you remove the sandwiches from the pan, cut them in half diagonally, sprinkle with a little more salt and serve them immediately.

Pizza toast

You can be as creative as you like with these cheat's pizzas and use up anything you have in your fridge. Alternatively, keep them simple and just use tomatoes, herbs, and cheese. They are great for lunch or a snack after school.

You will need

12 cherry tomatoes (look out for yellow ones as well as red ones)

4 handfuls of grated Cheddar cheese

4 thick slices of bread (or French baguette)

about 4 tablespoons tomato sauce (passata)

optional toppings e.g. chopped ham, canned tuna, canned corn, or chopped bell peppers

a handful of fresh parsley or other fresh herb, or a pinch of dried oregano

baking sheet

oven gloves

(makes 4 toasts)

1 Place the tomatoes on a chopping board and, with your hand in the bridge position, cut each one in half.

2 Grate Cheddar cheese onto a plate until you have about 4 handfuls.

3 Ask an adult to help you turn on the broiler (grill.) Put the bread slices on a baking sheet (if you need to slice your bread first see page 12.) Using oven gloves, put the baking sheet under the broiler (grill) and toast the bread until it is golden on one side. Watch it carefully so that it doesn't burn. Ask an adult to help you take the sheet out of the broiler (grill) and put it down on a board or trivet. Leave the toast to cool slightly.

4 Being careful, in case the baking sheet is still hot, turn the toast over, and spread the untoasted side with tomato sauce (passata.)

5 Arrange the tomato halves on top. If you want to add some of the other optional toppings, scatter them over the top now.

6 Using scissors, snip the herbs into small pieces and sprinkle over the top or sprinkle on a pinch of dried oregano instead.

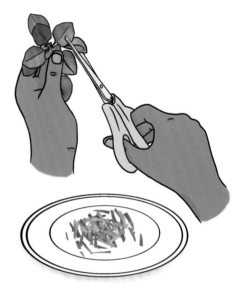

7 Sprinkle with the grated cheese and ask an adult to help you put the baking sheet back under the broiler (grill) until the cheese has melted.

Cheat's PIZZA!

Spicy couscous salad

This is an exciting, spicy salad which uses flavors and ingredients from the Middle East. With all these different ingredients it is a vegetarian meal in itself. It's easy too—once you have prepared the ingredients, there is very little cooking to do.

You will need

a 14 oz (400 g) can of chickpeas

a small can of corn kernels (sweetcorn)

2 carrots

2 scallions (spring onions)

2 tomatoes

1 lemon

1 heaping cup (200 g) couscous

a pinch each of ground cumin, coriander, and turmeric

about 1½ cups (350 ml) vegetable boullion (stock) or boullion (stock) cube/concentrate

a handful of baby spinach

1 tablespoon olive oil

colander

lemon squeezer

plastic wrap (clingfilm)

(serves 4)

You need to use a sharp knife quite a lot in this salad. Remember to hold your hand in the bridge position (page 11) when cutting larger fruits and vegetables like tomatoes in half, and claw position (page 11) when chopping or slicing foods.

1 Open the can of chickpeas and the can of corn and drain them through a colander.

2 Use a sharp knife and cut both ends of the carrots. Now peel them with a potato peeler like this: hold a carrot at one end and rest the other end on the chopping board. Starting halfway down, run the peeler down the carrot away from your body. Turn the carrot a little and peel the next strip. Keep turning and peeling until it is peeled all the way around. Now turn the carrot up the other way while you peel the other half.

3 Grate the carrots onto a small plate.

4 With a small sharp knife, trim the hairy roots off the scallions (spring onions.) Next, trim off the very dark green tops. Finally cut them into thin slices.

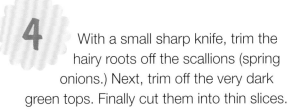

5 Cut the tomato in half with a sharp knife. Lay the two halves flat on the board and cut them into small chunks.

6 Cut the lemon in half with a sharp knife. Squeeze the juice from one half only with a lemon squeezer.

7 Measure out the couscous and pour it into a bowl. Add good pinches of the three spices and stir through the couscous.

8 If you have some vegetable boullion (stock) ask an adult to help you heat it up until it is boiling. If you are using cubes or concentrate, ask an adult to help you boil a kettle and carefully pour 1½ cups (350 ml) of boiling water into a measuring jug. Add the correct amount of cube/concentrate, (look at the instructions on the packet) and stir until the boullion (stock) has dissolved.

9 Ask an adult to help you pour the boiling vegetable boullion (stock) over the couscous —there should be enough boullion (stock) to just cover it. Give it a stir, then cover with plastic wrap (clingfilm) and leave to stand for 5 minutes. After 5 minutes, the couscous should have absorbed all of the boullion (stock.) Stir it around with a fork to make the couscous grains nice and fluffy.

Couscous is COOL!

10 Tip in all the other ingredients you have prepared—chickpeas, corn, carrots, scallions (spring onions,) tomato, and lemon juice. Add a handful of baby spinach and a tablespoon of olive oil. Mix together and serve!

Summer vegetable salad

This is a wonderful summer salad which tastes even better if you have dug up the potatoes and picked the peas, beans, and lettuce from your own garden. To make it even more delicious you could try adding canned tuna, olives, and tomatoes so it is a bit like a French "salade Niçoise".

You will need

1 lb (450 g) small new potatoes

4 eggs

14 oz (400 g) fresh peas in the pods (or 1 cup of frozen peas)

about 20 (200 g) green (French) beans

a few handfuls of lettuce leaves

2 tablespoons olive oil

2 teaspoons red wine or cider vinegar

3 saucepans

vegetable steamer (optional)

salad bowl

glass jar

(serves 4)

For this recipe you will need to boil potatoes, eggs, and beans in three different pans. Always ask an adult to help you with anything involving boiling water as it is very easy to scald yourself with boiling water and with steam.

1 Scrub the new potatoes with a vegetable brush. With your hand in the bridge position, cut any larger ones in half so they are all about the same size. Ask an adult to help you with all the next stages of boiling the potatoes: put a pan half-filled with water on the stovetop (hob) to boil. When it is boiling put in the potatoes. They will take about 15–20 minutes to cook depending on how big they are. To check if they are ready, test them with a knife—when they are cooked it should slide in easily. Once they are ready, drain them in a colander in the sink. Then put them into a big salad bowl.

2 While the potatoes are cooking, ask an adult to help you hard-boil the eggs. Put another pan half filled with water on the stovetop (hob.) When the water is boiling, lower each egg gently into the boiling water with a slotted spoon. Set the timer for 7 minutes.

3 When the timer pings, drain the eggs in a colander in the sink, then pour cold water over them to cool them down. When the eggs are really cold, peel off their shells. Using the bridge cutting technique (see page 11,) cut the eggs into quarters. Add them to the salad bowl.

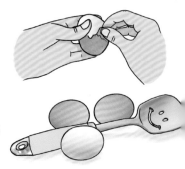

4 While the eggs are cooking and cooling, shell the peas into a small bowl.

5 Use a pair of kitchen scissors to cut both ends off all the beans.

6 Ask an adult to help you cook the beans and peas: put another pan of water on to boil. If you have a steamer, put the beans into the steamer, and set that over the boiling water. After about 8 minutes tip in the peas. Steam for another 2 minutes until both beans and peas are tender. (If you don't have a steamer, tip them straight into the water instead—they will take slightly less time to cook, but the beans will still take much longer than the peas.) Remove the steamer from the pan or drain the peas and beans through a colander into the sink.

7 Add the beans, peas and lettuce to the salad bowl— tear the lettuce leaves into smaller pieces if they are very big.

8 Measure the oil and vinegar into a jar. Add a small pinch of salt and a grind or two of pepper. Put the lid on the jar tightly, and give it a good shake. Add the dressing to the salad and gently toss together with a spoon and fork.

Butter-baked corn-on-the-cob

Corn is one of the best treats of the summer—bite into the sweet grains and let the butter run down your chin. Some people are neat corn eaters and nibble every grain carefully as they go—others are untidy and munch little bits all over the place. Which are you? You don't always have to cook corn in boiling water. Barbecuing is good, but roasting in the oven is just wonderful.

You will need

enough corn cobs for you and your family or friends (one per person)

a slice from a stick of unsalted butter for each cob (about 2 scant tablespoons/ 25 g)

salt and freshly ground black pepper

microwave or small saucepan

ovenproof dish big enough to fit the corn in a single layer

metal cooking tongs

oven gloves

timer

1 Ask an adult to help you preheat the oven to 400°F (200°C) Gas 6.

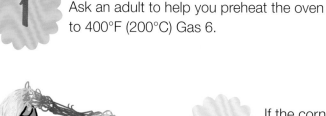

2 If the corn still has its green leafy covering, it must be shucked—pull off the leaves from the pointy top end, then pull off all the silky hairs. (If you want the corn in smaller pieces, ask an adult to help you cut them in half, as the cobs are quite tough and difficult to cut.)

3 Ask an adult to help you melt the butter. Cut a slice of butter for each corn cob with a table knife. Either put the butter in a small saucepan over the lowest possible heat, or put it in a microwave-proof dish and microwave on MEDIUM for about 20 seconds. Check, stir and heat again for another 20 seconds. Keep going like this until it has melted.

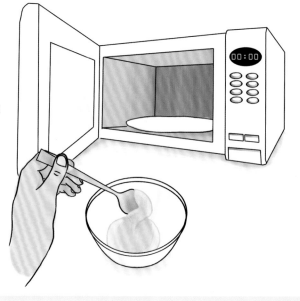

4 Pour the melted butter into the baking dish and add a pinch of salt and a good grind of pepper for each corn cob.

5 Put the corn cobs into the dish then roll each one in the butter mix so they are all well coated.

6 Put on oven gloves and ask an adult to help you put the corn to cook in the heated oven—this will take 30 minutes, but they will need to be turned during cooking, so set the timer for ten minutes. When the timer pings, put on oven gloves and ask an adult to help you turn the corn over—metal cooking tongs are the best thing to use. Set the timer for ten minutes again and when it pings turn the corn again. Set the timer for ten more minutes and this time, when it pings, the corn will be ready and lightly browned all over.

7 Put on oven gloves and ask an adult to help you take the dish out of the oven and put it on a board or trivet. The corn will be too hot to eat immediately, so let it stand for 5–10 minutes until the cobs are cool enough to pick up.

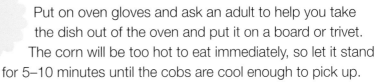

Do you MUNCH or NIBBLE your corn on the cob?

Pea and Parmesan risotto

A risotto is a bit like savory rice pudding! Risottos are simple to make, but you do need to stir the special Arborio rice (which is sometimes called Italian risotto rice) all the time as it cooks, so you need to be patient. You could flavor your risotto with other ingredients such as bacon, fava (broad) beans, mushrooms, or herbs instead of peas, but peas are easy as they don't need to be cooked first.

You will need

3¼ cups (750 ml) vegetable boullion (stock) or boullion (stock) powder, cubes or concentrate

1 medium onion

2 garlic cloves

2 tablespoons virgin olive oil

1½ cups (300 g) Italian Arborio rice

¾ cup (120 g) shelled fresh or frozen peas

1 tablespoon (15g) unsalted butter

salt and freshly ground black pepper

1 cup (100 g) grated Parmesan cheese

a few sprigs of parsley

a heavy-based medium saucepan (nonstick is best)

ladle

(serves 4)

1 First make up some hot boullion (stock.) Ask an adult to help you boil a kettle. Pour 3¼ cups (750 ml) of the hot water into a measuring pitcher (jug) and add the correct amount powder, cubes or concentrate according to the instructions on the packet. Stir it until it has dissolved.

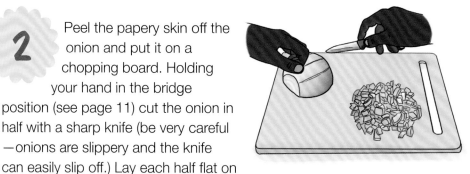

2 Peel the papery skin off the onion and put it on a chopping board. Holding your hand in the bridge position (see page 11) cut the onion in half with a sharp knife (be very careful —onions are slippery and the knife can easily slip off.) Lay each half flat on the board, trim off any hairy roots, and then cut into very small pieces. Push the pieces to one end of the board.

3 Put the garlic cloves on the other end and crush them slightly with the end of a rolling pin—the outside skin will split and will peel off easily. Chop the garlic into very tiny pieces.

Easy, peasy, cheesy RISOTTO

4 If your Parmesan needs grating (you can buy it ready-grated) carefully grate it onto a small plate using the finest holes on your cheese grater.

5 Measure out the correct quantity of rice and peas.

6 Now you are ready to cook. Put a medium, heavy-based saucepan on the stovetop (hob) and pour in the olive oil.

7 Ask an adult to help you turn on the stovetop (hob) to very low heat and slide the chopped onions and garlic off the board into the pan. Stir them to cover them in oil then cook gently for about 10 minutes. The onion should turn clear and not go brown. Stir them every few minutes to make sure that they don't stick.

8 Stir in the rice (don't wash it first,) then stir in the peas. Turn up the heat to medium, and add a ladle of the hot vegetable boullion (stock.) Stir gently so it doesn't splash you, and as soon as the liquid is absorbed by the rice, add another ladle of stock.

9 Keep on stirring the rice very gently the whole time so it doesn't stick to the bottom or sides of the pan, and keep on adding the hot stock one ladle at a time. It will take about 20 minutes of stirring before the rice is tender. Taste a few grains with a teaspoon, but let it cool first so you don't burn your mouth. The mixture should be creamy and moist, not dry or very wet and soupy—the exact amount of stock you will need depends on the brand of rice you use, and how fast the rice is cooking.

10 As soon as the rice is tender (not hard any more, but not too soft,) turn off the heat. Add the butter, salt and pepper, and half of the grated cheese. Stir everything gently into the rice, then cover the pan and leave for 4–5 minutes.

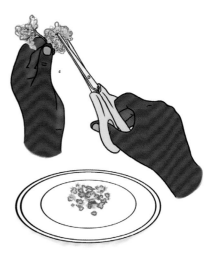

11 Rinse the parsley sprigs and snip them with kitchen scissors. Uncover the pan, sprinkle the parsley on top, then serve immediately with the extra grated cheese.

Spanish omelet

This is a great recipe to make when you have some leftover potatoes from another meal, otherwise you will need to cook a potato first (you could ask an adult to help you do this quickly in a microwave.) You can change this basic recipe using your favorite bits and pieces from the refrigerator. The main thing is to add plenty of vegetables, though you can also add strips of ham, pepperoni, or cooked turkey.

You will need

2 tablespoons grated Cheddar cheese

2 scallions (spring onions)

1 medium tomato

½ red or green bell pepper or zucchini (courgette)

2 tablespoons peas—cooked or frozen

2 tablespoons corn kernels (sweetcorn)—cooked, frozen, or canned

1 cooked potato

3 large eggs

1½ tablespoons cream (any kind)

a pinch of salt

a pinch of pepper

1½ tablespoons olive oil

cheese grater

nonstick skillet (frying pan)

(serves 2)

1 Grate the cheese onto a small plate.

2 Wash the vegetables in a colander and place them on a chopping board. With a small sharp knife, trim the hairy roots off the scallions (spring onions.) Next, trim off the very dark green tops. Finally cut them into thin slices.

3 Holding your hand in the bridge position (see page 11,) cut the tomato in half with a sharp knife. Lay the two halves flat on the board and cut them into small chunks.

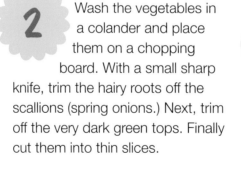

A ONE-PAN supper dish!

4 If you are using a bell pepper, hold it firmly on the board and, using a small, sharp knife, carefully cut around the stalk and then pull it out, along with the core and all the seeds. Throw these away and rinse off any seeds still inside under a faucet (tap.) Now, holding your hand in the bridge position, cut the pepper in half. Put one half back in the fridge and, with your hand in the claw position, carefully slice the other half into strips. If you are using a zucchini (courgette) instead, cut this into slices.

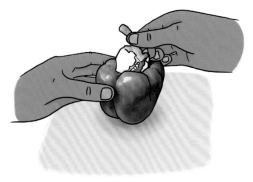

5 Measure the peas and corn kernels (sweetcorn) into a bowl and cut the cooked potato into small cubes, the size of dice.

6 Break the eggs into a medium bowl. To do this tap each one firmly on the side of the bowl to crack it. (Not too hard or you will smash it completely!) Then put your thumbs into the crack and pull the two halves apart. Scoop out any pieces of shell with another bigger piece of shell. Add the cream, cheese, salt, and pepper and mix well with a fork.

7 Now you are ready to cook. Put the olive oil in a nonstick skillet (frying pan) and ask an adult to help you to warm it gently over low heat.

8 Add the onions, tomato, peas, and corn to the oil and stir well with a wooden spoon. Cook these gently for a few minutes, then add the bell pepper or zucchini and the potato to the pan and stir well.

9 Let the vegetables cook for 2 more minutes, then stir again and pour in the egg mix. Stir the whole mixture gently once, then turn up the heat to medium and let the omelet cook until the eggs look almost set, and are no longer runny on the surface.

10 Ask an adult to help you remove the pan from the heat and slide the omelet out of the pan and onto a serving platter. Cut into wedges and eat immediately.

Oven-baked herby burgers

Lots of children have helped to choose the recipes in this book. They all felt that the book should have a burger recipe in it and they found this oven-baked burger recipe easy to cook and good to eat. Burgers like this would be great to make when your friends come around for a party or sleepover.

You will need

a little olive or vegetable oil

1 in. cube (30 g) Cheddar cheese

small handful of fresh herbs, such as parsley, cilantro (coriander,) or thyme

2 scallions (spring onions)

1 free-range egg

1 lb 2 oz (500 g) good-quality ground beef (mince)—don't buy extra-lean beef—otherwise your burger will be too dry

lettuce

tomatoes

8 bread rolls

tomato ketchup

pastry brush

baking sheet

oven gloves

(makes 8)

1 Ask an adult to help you turn the oven on to 375°F (190°C) Gas 5. Dip a pastry brush into a little olive or vegetable oil and brush it all over a baking sheet. This will stop the burgers from sticking to the sheet.

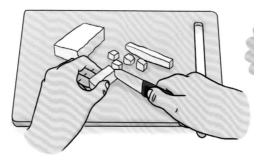

2 Using a table knife, cut the cheese into small pieces on a chopping board.

Tip:

To make lamb burgers, swap the beef for lamb and add thyme leaves, plus snipped dried apricots instead of Cheddar cheese.

3 Using scissors, snip the herbs into small pieces and put into a mixing bowl. Throw away any tough stalks. Still using scissors, snip the hairy roots and the dark green leaves off the scallions (spring onions) and throw them away, then snip the scallions into tiny pieces and put in the bowl.

PERFECT *party food!*

4 Now you need to crack open the egg: to do this, tap it firmly on the edge of a small bowl to crack it. (Not too hard or you will smash it completely!) Put your thumbs into the crack and pull the egg shell apart. Scoop out any pieces of shell using a bigger piece of shell as a scoop. Mix with a fork.

5 Put the ground beef (mince,) chopped cheese, and egg into the mixing bowl with the herbs and onions and mix everything together really well with your clean hands.

6 Break the beef mixture in half and then break each piece in half again to make 4 pieces. Now break each quarter in half again to make 8 pieces. Roll each piece into a ball with your hands, then put onto the oiled baking sheet and flatten into a burger shape. Now, WASH YOUR HANDS—you must always wash your hands with plenty of soap and hot water after handling raw meat.

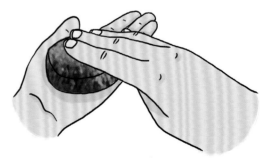

7 Ask an adult to help you put the baking sheet into the oven using oven gloves. Cook for 8 minutes and then ask an adult to help you take the sheet out of the oven. Using a spatula, turn the burgers over and put back in the oven for 8 more minutes or until cooked in the middle.

8 While the burgers are cooking, prepare the salad. Pull a few leaves off the lettuce, put them in a colander and wash them under the saucet (tap.) Dry them in a salad spinner or shake them well in the colander.

9 Take the tomato and, holding your hand in the bridge position (see page 10) cut it in half with a small sharp knife. Lay the two halves flat on the board and cut them into slices.

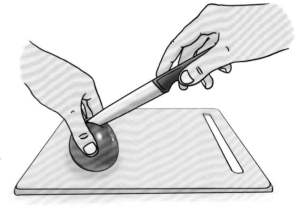

10 Ask an adult to help you take the burgers out of the oven. Eat in bread rolls with lettuce, tomatoes and ketchup.

Italian roast chicken

It's hard to resist the smell of roasting chicken! This dish uses chicken pieces, so there's no difficult carving to do and the gravy appears during cooking. You can make this with whole chicken legs or with thigh, but try to use organic or free-range chicken pieces if you can.

You will need

4 chicken legs or thighs

4 unpeeled garlic cloves

1 large lemon

2 tablespoons olive oil

salt and freshly ground black pepper

4 large sprigs fresh thyme or rosemary

ovenproof baking dish, big enough to hold the chicken in one layer

lemon squeezer

(serves 4)

1 Ask an adult to help you preheat the oven to 425°F (220°C) Gas 7.

2 Put the chicken pieces into the ovenproof dish, skin side facing up. Check that they don't overlap each other. When you've done this, wash your hands thoroughly with soap and hot water. You should also wash thoroughly any boards or work surfaces which have been touched by the raw chicken. This is important to avoid the spread of bacteria which could make you ill.

3 Put the garlic cloves into the dish between the chicken pieces. Hold the lemon on a chopping board with your hand in the bridge position, and cut it in half. Squeeze the juice from each half with a lemon squeezer. Use a teaspoon to spoon the juice over the chicken pieces spreading it around all over the skin.

4 Pour half a tablespoon of oil over the top of each chicken piece so the skin is evenly coated in oil.

Mmmm CHICKEN!

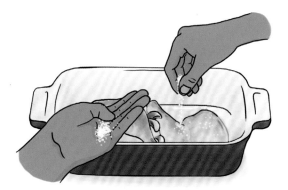

5 Sprinkle each chicken piece with a pinch of salt and then about three turns of the pepper grinder.

6 Finally, set a sprig of thyme or rosemary on the top of each piece of chicken.

7 Put on oven gloves and ask an adult to help you put the baking dish into the heated oven. Set the timer for 40 minutes for large legs, and 35 minutes for thighs. As the chicken cooks, the legs become a crispy golden brown, surrounded by a light brown cooking-juice gravy. When the chicken is done, ask an adult to remove the dish from the hot oven and put it onto the table to serve.

Pasta with beans and bacon

You know summer is in full swing when fresh fava (broad) beans appear in the supermarket. They are best fresh and it is fun to pod them, but you could use frozen beans instead. They are delicious mixed with bacon and grated cheese and stirred into pasta.

You will need

2¾ lb (1.3 kg) fresh fava (broad) beans in their pods (or 12 oz/350g frozen beans)

1 garlic clove

7 oz (200 g) good-quality chopped bacon—look out for lardons or pancetta cubes (these are slightly smoked)

¾ cup (170 ml) heavy (double) cream

14 oz (400 g) dried pasta (this sauce works really well with spaghetti or linguine)

fresh basil or mint leaves (optional)

salt and freshly ground black pepper

grated Parmesan, to serve

rolling pin

skillet (frying pan)

timer

large saucepan

(serves 4)

1 Shell the fava (broad) beans by splitting the pods and pulling out the beans.

2 Put the garlic cloves on a chopping board and lightly crush them with a rolling pin—the outside skin will split and will peel off easily. It will also help to release the garlicky flavor into the sauce.

3 Ask an adult to help you put a skillet (frying pan) on the stovetop (hob) over high heat. Add the bacon bits and fry for 1 minute. Turn the heat down, add the clove of garlic and fry, stirring with a wooden spoon, until the bacon is cooked and just beginning to go slightly crisp.

4 Add the heavy (double) cream and stir. Turn off the heat and leave the skillet (frying pan) to one side.

5 Ask an adult to help you cook the pasta. Bring a large saucepan of water to a boil and add a pinch of salt. Once the pasta water is boiling, add the pasta, give it a stir and keep the heat high until the water boils again, then turn it down a little so the water doesn't boil over the top of the saucepan—but make sure it keeps boiling. Set a timer for the cooking time shown on the package.

6 Four minutes before the timer is due to go off, add the fava (broad) beans to the pasta pan so that they cook with the pasta.

7 When the timer pings, take out a piece of pasta with a slotted spoon. Let it cool for a moment and then taste to see if it is cooked. It should be "al dente," which means soft with a slight firmness in the middle. If it is still hard, cook for a little longer and test again. When it is cooked, ask an adult to help you drain the pasta and beans through a colander. Then tip them back into the empty pasta pan.

8 Now add the fresh herbs to the cream sauce, (if you are using them,) tearing the leaves up into smaller pieces as you drop them in. Season the sauce with black pepper. You shouldn't need salt as the bacon is salty, but taste it to check.

9 Add the sauce to the pan with the cooked pasta and broad beans. Ask an adult to help you heat it up gently over low heat until warmed through, mixing occasionally.

10 Sprinkle the Parmesan cheese over the top and serve.

How many BEANS fit in one pod?

Pasta butterflies with zucchini (courgettes)

If you are vegetarian, or you are cooking for vegetarian friends or family, this is a really useful pasta recipe to learn. You don't need many ingredients, and there's a good chance you already have things like golden raisins (sultanas) and pine nuts in your kitchen cupboard. You will have two pans cooking together in this recipe, which will test your cooking skills!

You will need

2 tablespoons golden raisins (sultanas)

1 unwaxed or organic lemon, washed

3 medium zucchini (courgettes)

2 garlic cloves

3 tablespoons olive oil

14 oz (400 g) dried farfalle (bow-tie) pasta

3 tablespoons pine nuts

salt and freshly ground black pepper

2 large saucepans

grater

garlic crusher

colander

(serves 4)

1 Put the golden raisins (sultanas) into a little dish. Ask an adult to help you boil a kettle and cover them with hot water. Leave them for about 15 minutes.

2 While they are soaking, carefully use the finest holes of a grater to grate the zest (yellow skin) off the lemon into a saucer.

3 Wash the zucchini (courgettes) and chop off the ends. Throw the ends away and cut the zucchini into thin slices using a small sharp knife—remember to keep your hand in the claw position.

4 Peel the garlic cloves and put them into a garlic crusher ready to use later. The golden raisins (sultanas) should be nice and plump by now, so drain them through a colander.

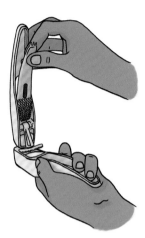

5 Now you are ready to cook. Ask an adult to help you heat the olive oil in a large saucepan, then put the zucchini to fry over medium heat for 6–8 minutes, until they are golden; you will need to give them a good stir now and again.

6 Once the zucchini are cooking, ask the adult to help you put a large pan of water to boil ready for the pasta. Add a pinch of salt. As soon as the water boils, pour in the pasta, give it a stir and keep the heat high until the water comes to a boil again, then turn it down a little so the water doesn't boil over the top of the saucepan—but make sure it keeps boiling. Set a timer for the cooking time shown on the package.

7 When the zucchini are ready, add the pine nuts and cook for another 2–3 minutes, until they are golden.

8 Crush the garlic into the zucchini and cook for just 2 minutes; you don't want it to cook so much that it browns, which is when it becomes bitter.

9 Add the golden raisins (sultanas) and lemon zest to the pan. Stir them into the mixture. Season the mixture with some salt and black pepper. Turn off the heat from under the pan.

10 When the timer pings, take out a piece of pasta with a slotted spoon. Let it cool for a moment and then taste to see if it is cooked. It should be "al dente" which means soft with a slight firmness in the middle. If it is still hard, cook for a little longer and test again. When it is cooked, ask an adult to help you drain the pasta through a colander.

Delicious VEGGIE pasta

11 Tip the pasta into the zucchini mixture and toss everything together using two wooden spoons/spatulas.

Pink pasta

Strips of smoked salmon turn the creamy sauce for this pasta a pretty pink. The snipped fresh chives or dill give it a stronger flavor, but you don't have to use them. This is a really easy recipe for a beginner to make, with no frying or cutting with sharp knives.

You will need

5 oz (150 g) smoked salmon or smoked trout (trimmings are fine)

4 tablespoons crème fraîche or heavy (double) cream

black pepper

10 oz (300 g) egg tagliatelle (fettuccine)

a small bunch of fresh chives or a few sprigs of dill

scissors

small saucepan

(serves 4)

1 To make the sauce, snip the smoked salmon into small strips using kitchen scissors, and put them in a small saucepan. (If you are using trimmings they are already small enough.)

2 Spoon in the crème fraîche or cream and then grind in about three grinds of pepper from the pepper mill.

3 Ask an adult to help you set the pan over the lowest possible heat. Warm the ingredients so the cream melts and the salmon turns a pale pink. Then turn off the heat under the pan.

4 Ask an adult to help you put a large pan of water on to boil ready for the pasta. Add a pinch of salt. As soon as the water boils, add the pasta, give it a stir and keep the heat high until the water comes to a boil again, then turn it down a little so the water doesn't boil over the top of the saucepan —but make sure it keeps boiling. Set a timer for the cooking time shown on the package.

Tip:

For one of your "five a day" add ½ cup (125 g) frozen peas or corn kernels (sweetcorn) to the sauce after you pour in the cream.

5 When the timer pings, ask an adult to remove about half a ladle (about three tablespoons) of water from the pasta pan and add it to the small pan with the sauce.

6 Then ask your adult helper to take out a piece of pasta with a spaghetti spoon. Let it cool for a moment so you don't burn your mouth and then taste to see if it is cooked. It should be "al dente" which means soft with a slight firmness in the middle. If it is still hard, cook it for a little longer and then check again. When it is done, ask an adult to help you drain the pasta through a colander.

7 Tip the pasta into a large serving bowl and pour the sauce over the top. Hold a fork in each hand and carefully lift and toss the pasta until it is well mixed with the sauce.

8 Using kitchen scissors, snip the chives or dill straight onto the pasta. Then serve with salad or green vegetables.

Pretty in PINK!

Roasted onions and sausages

This is perfect food for Halloween or fall parties. In this recipe, there is a lot of putting things in a hot oven and taking them out again. Always wear oven gloves when you do this. Even when putting a cold dish in the oven, it easy to burn your arm on the hot shelves.

You will need

4 medium baking potatoes

2 red or white onions, or one of each color

a little olive oil

4 eating apples

12 good-quality chipolatas or other sausages

vegetable brush

large roasting tin

tongs

(serves 4)

1 Ask an adult to turn the oven on to 400°F (200°C) Gas 6.

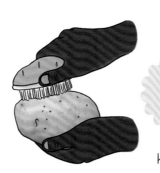

2 Use a brush to scrub any dirt off the baking potatoes and then scoop off any knobbly "eyes" or bad bits with a table knife. Pierce them each once with a sharp knife to make sure that they don't explode in the oven. Remember to put on oven gloves then ask an adult to help you put them on the shelf in the oven.

3 Peel the papery skin off the onions but don't cut off the root end. You need this to stop the wedges from falling apart. Hold one onion on a chopping board with your hand in the bridge position and cut it in half cutting from top to bottom so that you cut through the root end. Lay the two halves flat on the board and cut them in half again so that you have 4 wedges, and then cut each wedge in half again. Do the same with the other onion. Scatter the wedges over a heavy-based roasting tin and use a spoon to sprinkle a little olive oil over them.

4 Using the bridge cutting technique, cut the apples in hal and then into quarters. Ask an adult to help you remove the cores by cutting a "V" shape into the center of each quarter. Scatter the apples in the roasting pan with the onion

5 Arrange the sausages on top of the apples and onions. Afterward wash your hands thoroughly with soap and water as you have been touching raw meat. Then sprinkle a little more olive oil over everything in the tin.

A cook-in-the oven FEAST!

6 Put on oven gloves and ask an adult to help you put the pan in the oven. Set a timer for 20 minutes. When it pings, ask an adult to help you take the hot pan out of the oven (use oven gloves) and put it on a board or trivet. Turn the sausages over with tongs so that they go brown on both sides. Use oven gloves to put the pan back in the oven for another 15 minutes—set the timer again.

7 Ask an adult to help you check that the potatoes are cooked. Ask them to lay a potato onto a flat surface with oven gloves, then push a sharp knife into the biggest potato. The potato should be soft all the way through. If the potatoes are done, take everything out of the oven and serve on plates.

Meatloaf

This is a good recipe for all you cooks who like getting your hands dirty, as all the mixing is done by hand. It is tasty served with some simple potato wedges and green vegetables or salad. A squirt of ketchup goes very well with this!

You will need

1 onion

2 garlic cloves

5 oz (150 g) Parmesan cheese

1 egg

2 lb (900 g) lean ground beef (mince)

2 teaspoons dried oregano

sea salt and freshly ground black pepper

a 8 x 4 x 2 in./1 lb (450 g) loaf pan

wax (greaseproof) paper

pencil

garlic crusher

(serves 6–8)

1 Put the loaf pan on a sheet of wax (greaseproof) paper and draw around the base. Cut out the rectangle and lay it in the bottom of the pan. This will help the meatloaf to turn out of the pan easily.

2 Ask an adult to help you turn the oven on to 350°F (180°C) Gas 4.

3 Peel the papery outside skin off the onion and put it on a chopping board. Holding your hand in the bridge position, cut the onion in half with a sharp knife. Be very careful—onions are slippery and the knife can easily slip off. Lay each half flat on the board, trim off any hairy roots, and now with your hand in the claw position, cut each half into small pieces. Put the onion into a large bowl.

4 Peel the garlic cloves and use a garlic crusher to crush them into the bowl.

A MEATY feast!

5 Use a cheese grater to grate the Parmesan onto a plate and add it to the bowl.

6 Break the egg into a small bowl. To do this, tap it firmly on the side of the bowl to crack it. (Not too hard or you will smash it completely!) Then put your thumbs into the crack and pull the two halves apart. Scoop out any pieces of shell with a bigger piece of egg shell, then beat with a fork until smooth.

7 Pour the egg into the bowl with the onion and garlic and add the ground (minced) beef and oregano. Season well with a good pinch of salt and three or four grinds of black pepper.

8 Now for the messy part! Put your clean hands right in the bowl and mix the ingredients with your fingers until everything is well mixed together. Then use your hands to scoop the mixture into the loaf pan. Smooth it down with your fingers.

9 Now, WASH YOUR HANDS—you must always wash your hands with plenty of soap and hot water after handling raw meat.

10 Put on oven gloves and ask an adult to help you put the pan in the oven. Set the timer for 45 minutes.

11 When the timer pings, ask an adult to remove the pan from the hot oven and put it down on a board. Put on oven gloves and loosen the meatloaf from around the edges of the pan with a palette knife, in case it has stuck, and then turn it upside down onto the board. The meatloaf should drop out neatly.

12 Use some tongs or a table knife to lift off the hot greaseproof paper. Cut the loaf into slices and serve.

Salmon on sticks

On a hot summer's day these salmon kebabs make an unusual, tasty and healthy alternative to burgers or sausages. Serve them with some green salad and new potatoes.

You will need

....

1 lb (450 g) cherry tomatoes

1¼ lb (600 g) boneless and skinless salmon fillet

a small bunch of fresh chives

2 small lemons

salt

3 tablespoons olive oil

12 bamboo skewers, about 12 in (30 cm) long large ovenproof dish

kitchen scissors

pastry brush

ridged stovetop grill pan

(makes about 12 skewers to serve 6 people)

1 Soak the skewers in an ovenproof dish of cold water for 30 minutes. This will stop them burning when you put them on the hot grill pan.

2 While they are soaking prepare the food: Wash the tomatoes in a colander.

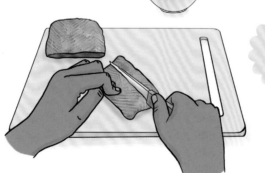

3 Ask an adult to help you cut the salmon into bite-size chunks—about 1½ in (3 cm) squares work well. Put the pieces into a large bowl.

4 Snip the chives into small pieces, straight into the bowl, using kitchen scissors.

5 Remembering to hold your hand in the bridge position, cut one lemon in half with a sharp knife. Squeeze the juice from half of the lemon with a lemon squeezer and pour it over the salmon. Cut the other half lemon in half again. Cut the second lemon into quarters. Put these 6 lemon quarters to one side for serving later.

6 Sprinkle two good pinches of salt into the bowl and give everything a mix with your clean hands to make sure all the pieces are covered with the lemon juice mixture. Now wash your hands thoroughly with soap and water.

7

Take a skewer and push on a chunk of salmon. Push it along until it is about 2 in (5cm) from the end and then push on a tomato. Continue pushing alternate pieces of salmon and tomato onto the skewer until there is about 2 in (5cm) of uncovered skewer left at the end. Do the same for the other skewers. You should end up with about 4 pieces of salmon and four tomatoes on each skewer. Wash your hands again.

8 Lay the skewers on a plate. Pour a little olive oil into a cup and use a pastry brush to brush oil all over the salmon and tomatoes.

9 Ask an adult to help you heat a ridged stovetop (hob) grill pan until it is quite hot. You will not be able to fit all the skewers into the pan at once so ask an adult to turn on the oven to 200°F (100°C) Gas ¼ and to put in an ovenproof dish where you can pop the cooked skewers to keep warm while the others are cooking. Ask an adult to help you put some of the skewers onto the hot grill pan and cook for about 3 minutes, then turn them over and cook them for another 2–3 minutes until the salmon is cooked through and golden brown. Put the first batch into the oven while you cook the next batch.

10 Serve with the lemon wedges to squeeze over.

Tip:

You could also cook these skewers on a barbecue—ask an adult to put them on the barbecue when it is hot enough. Cook them in the same way, cooking for 5–6 minutes, turning them over once halfway through cooking until the salmon is cooked through and golden brown.

What else could you cook on **STICKS?**

Beef and corn tortilla tubes

These are lots of fun to make and eat! The corn tortillas become lovely and crisp when you bake them in the oven. (You will need to use corn tortillas, not flour ones.) If you like your Mexican food hot and spicy, add some Tabasco sauce to the mixture.

You will need

1 red onion

3 carrots

1 garlic clove

1 tablespoon olive oil, plus a little extra

1 lb 2 oz (500 g) ground beef (mince)

1 lb 2 oz (500 g) tomato sauce (passata)

pinch brown sugar

Tabasco sauce (optional)

8 corn tortillas

garlic crusher

skillet (frying pan) with a lid

wooden spoon

pastry brush

large rectangular ovenproof dish

oven gloves

(makes 8)

1 Ask an adult to help you to turn the oven on to 375°F (190°C) Gas 5.

2 Peel the papery outside skin off the onion and put it on a chopping board. Holding your hand in the bridge position, cut the onion in half with a small sharp knife. Be very careful—onions are slippery and the knife can easily slip off. Lay each half flat on the board, trim off any hairy roots, and now with your hand in the claw position, cut each half into thin slices.

3 Use a brush to scrub the carrots well under the faucet (tap) then grate them with the biggest holes of the grater.

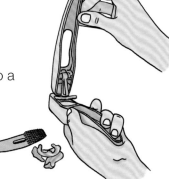

4 Peel the garlic and put it into a garlic press ready to use.

5 Put a tablespoon of oil, the onion, and carrots into a heavy-based skillet (frying pan) and crush the garlic straight into the pan. Ask an adult to help you put it over low heat on the stovetop (hob.) Heat gently until the vegetables are soft. This will take 10 minutes or more. Stir them occasionally as they cook.

TASTY tortillas!

6 Add the beef, raise the heat a little, and fry for 10 minutes, or until the meat is turning golden brown. Add the tomato sauce (passata) and a pinch of sugar (and, if you like your tortillas spicy, a few shakes of Tabasco sauce.) Cover the pan with a lid, turn down the heat again, and cook gently for another 10 minutes. The mixture will be quite dry, which is what you want. Turn off the heat. Let the pan cool for a few minutes so that you don't burn yourself when rolling the tortillas.

7 Roughly divide the mixture into eight portions in the skillet (frying pan.) Lay a tortilla on the chopping board, then spoon a portion of beef along the middle. Roll the tortilla around the beef and lift it carefully into an ovenproof dish. Do the same for the other tortillas.

8 Pour a small amount of olive oil into a cup. Use a pastry brush to brush the tortilla tubes with a little oil. Put on oven gloves and ask an adult to help you put the dish into the oven and cook for 15 minutes.

Desserts

Fruit salad on a stick

These fruit salads on sticks are guaranteed to make the juice run down your chin! You can use any fruits, as long as they are big enough to thread onto bamboo skewers (best not to try with blueberries!) Choose a good mix of colors and textures like the kiwi fruit, bananas, nectarines, and strawberries used here—although you could make tropical sticks with fruits like pineapple, mango, starfruit, and melon.

You will need

2 kiwi fruit

1 large or 2 small bananas

1 peach or nectarine

16 strawberries

vegetable peeler

8 bamboo skewers

(serves 4)

1 Peel the kiwi fruit with a vegetable peeler. Start at the top and run the vegetable peeler around the fruit, turning it as you go to create a spiral of peel. See if you can make a really long spiral!

2 Put the kiwi fruit on a clean board and use the bridge cutting technique to cut it in half (see page 11.) Turn the halves cut side down onto the board, and with your hand in the claw position (see page 11) cut each half into two wedges.

Tip:

Remember when you are cutting up fruit to use the bridge technique (see page 11) for cutting large, round pieces of fruit in half. To slice fruit, use the claw technique (see page 11)—that way your fingers will be safe!

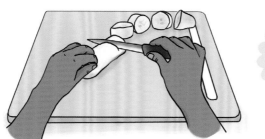

3 Peel the banana(s) and cut into a total of eight chunks.

4

Rinse the peach or nectarine under a cold faucet (tap.) Again, use the bridge-cutting technique to cut the peach in half, but this time cut downward until you reach the pit (stone,) then turn the fruit, cutting as you go, until it is cut through to the pit (stone) all the way around. Twist the two halves and, if you are lucky, they will pull apart. Pull out the pit (stone,) then turn the halves cut side down on the board and slice each half into four wedges. (If the halves won't twist apart, you will have to slice the fruit carefully off the pit (stone.)

Choose your FAVORITE fruits

5 Wipe the strawberries with a soft cloth and pull out the green leafy tops (or you can leave them in to look pretty.)

6 Carefully thread the fruit onto the skewers starting and finishing with a strawberry. Each skewer will have two strawberries, a wedge each of kiwi fruit and peach, and a chunk of banana.

Plum crumble

Everyone loves a crumble for dessert. This is a recipe for plum crumble, but you can sprinkle the crumble mix on top of many different fruits—apple, blackberry, raspberry, rhubarb, plum, peach, nectarine—whatever is in season is best because it will be cheap and plentiful to buy. Fresh or frozen berries are easiest to use as you don't need to chop them up.

You will need

For the fruit filling:

seasonal fruit e.g., 15 plums or about 1¼ lb (600 g) fresh or frozen berries or about 12 peaches or nectarines

4 tablespoons orange juice

3 tablespoons light brown soft sugar

1 level tablespoon all-purpose (plain) flour

For the crumble topping:

½ stick (100 g) unsalted butter, chilled

1 heaping cup (150 g) all-purpose (plain flour)

2 handfuls oats (or muesli if you prefer)

4 tablespoons light brown soft sugar

1 teaspoon ground cinnamon or mixed spice

large ovenproof dish

(serves 4–6)

1 Ask an adult to help you turn the oven on to 350°F (180°C) Gas 4.

2 Rinse the plums in a colander under a cold faucet (tap.) Use the bridge cutting technique (see page 11) to cut downward into each plum until you reach the pit (stone.) Then turn the fruit, cutting as you go, until it is cut through to the pit (stone) all the way around. Pull the two halves apart and take out the pit (stone.)

3 Put the plums into a large ovenproof dish. Pour the orange juice over them, add the sugar and flour, and mix with a spoon.

4

To make the topping, take the butter out of the fridge and put it onto a chopping board. Use a table knife to cut it up into small cubes.

What **FRUIT** is in season now?

5

Put the flour into a bowl and add the butter. Using both clean hands, pick up small amounts of butter and flour and rub them together between your thumbs and forefingers. Keep picking up more of the mixture and rubbing it together. In this way the butter gradually gets mixed into the flour until there are no lumps left and the mixture looks like breadcrumbs. This can take a few minutes.

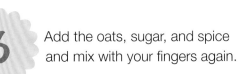

6   Add the oats, sugar, and spice and mix with your fingers again.

7   Use your fingers to sprinkle the mixture evenly over the top of the plums. Now wash your hands. Ask an adult to help you put the dish into the oven using oven gloves. Bake for 25–30 minutes, or until the crumble topping is crisp, the plums are soft, and the fruit juices are bubbling up around the edges.

Sparkling fruit jellies

Jelly and ice cream are perfect to serve at parties, and these sparkling fruit jellies are nothing like the plain red, wobbly kind you often get. Look out for sparkling fruit juices to make these party pieces. Whisking the jelly, just before it sets, traps the bubbles in the jelly, which gives them some extra "fizz".

You will need

8 leaves of gelatin

3¼ cups (750 ml) either sparkling grape, raspberry, or cranberry juice, or pomegranate lemonade

3–4 tablespoons superfine (caster) sugar

1 pomegranate

¾ cup (100 g) seedless red grapes

¾ cup (100 g) blueberries

wire whisk

plastic wrap (clingfilm)

(serves 6–8)

1 Put the gelatin leaves in a bowl of cold water and leave them to soak for 5 minutes. This will soften them.

2 Measure out 1 cup (250 ml) of the sparkling juice and pour it into a saucepan. Add the sugar. Ask an adult to help you put it over medium heat. Stir it to dissolve the sugar, and then heat it until it is beginning to bubble, but not yet boiling. Take the pan off the heat.

3 Take the gelatin leaves out of the water, squeeze them out a bit and add them to the hot juice. Stir it until the gelatin is completely dissolved.

Jellies with FIZZ!

 4 Pour the remaining sparkling juice into a large bowl, add the hot juice and gelatin mixture, and mix together well with a wire whisk. Put the bowl in the fridge. Set a timer for one hour.

5 While the jelly is in the fridge, prepare the fruit. Pomegranates are strange in that you only eat the seeds (pips.) To get them out, use a sharp knife to cut the pomegranate open across its middle, remembering to have your hand in the bridge position (see page 11) as you cut—they are quite tough so you may need to ask an adult to help you with this. Then, hold one half over a bowl, cut-side down and bash the skin with a rolling pin or wooden spoon. The seeds should pop out. Do the same with the other half. Pick out any bits of white pith, as these are bitter. You can use a pin to pull out any seeds from the pomegranate which don't pop out. Take about five tablespoons of seeds out of the bowl and put them in a saucer to use for decoration later.

6 Wash the grapes in a colander, under a cold faucet (tap,) and then cut each of them in half – remember to have your hand in the bridge position for this. Add the grapes to the bowl with the pomegranate seeds.

7 Wash the blueberries in a colander, under a cold faucet (tap,) and put them into the bowl with the other fruit. Mix them together.

8 When the timer pings, check to see if the jelly is beginning to set. It may take longer than this, but don't forget it and let it get too firm. Once the jelly has started to set, you need to make it bubbly. Quickly whisk the jelly with a wire whisk to make air bubbles.

9 Tip the fruit into the jelly and fold it in with a big metal spoon—folding means carefully cutting through the mixture with the edge of the spoon, working in a kind of figure eight. Work carefully because you don't want to squash the fruit as you mix it in, or squash the bubbles out of the jelly.

10 Divide the jelly between 6–8 small glasses. Cover with plastic wrap (clingfilm) and chill in the fridge until completely set.

11 Use the pomegranate seeds you set aside earlier to decorate the jellies before you serve them.

Peach and mascarpone dessert

This is a lovely dessert to have in the summer, when juicy, ripe peaches are at their best—but it works well with other fruit too. Try it with raspberries and strawberries, or even chopped ripe pears in the winter.

You will need

4 ripe peaches

½ cup (100g) plus 1 tablespoon sugar

1 unwaxed lemon

8 oz (225 g) mascarpone

2 extra-large egg whites

4 sprigs of fresh mint, to garnish

electric beater (whisk)

(serves 4)

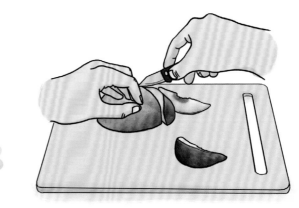

1

Rinse the peaches under a cold faucet (tap.) Use the bridge cutting technique (see page 11) to cut each peach in half, but only cut downward until you reach the pit (stone,) then turn the fruit, cutting as you go, until it is cut through to the pit (stone) all the way around. Twist the two halves and, if you are lucky, they will pull apart. Pull out the pit (stone,) then turn the halves cut side down on the board. Chop the flesh into small chunks and place them in a bowl (If the halves won't twist apart, you will have to slice the fruit carefully off the pit [stone].) Stir in 1 tablespoon of the sugar.

2 Wash the lemon and, carefully, use the finest holes of a grater to grate the zest (yellow skin) off the lemon into a saucer. Stir the zest in with the peaches.

BURSTING with summer flavors!

3 In a separate bowl, using a wooden spoon, beat the mascarpone and remaining sugar together until they are smooth. Beat means stir hard and quickly!

4 Now separate the egg whites from the yolks. To do this, carefully break one egg at a time onto a flat plate, place an egg cup over the yolk, and then let the white slide off into a very clean mixing bowl leaving the yolk behind. You do not need the yolks for this recipe, so put them into a cup to use for something else.

5 Ask an adult to help you whisk the egg whites with an electric beater (whisk.) Whisk until they turn into a stiff white foam. You'll know you have whisked enough if, when you lift out the beater (whisk,) there are sharp little peaks of white standing up in the bowl.

6 Take 2 tablespoons of the egg whites and beat them into the mascarpone to make it less stiff. Then fold the remaining egg whites into the mascarpone using a big metal spoon. Folding means carefully cutting through the mixture with the edge of the spoon, working in a kind of figure eight so you don't squash the air bubbles out of the egg white.

7 Spoon some of the peaches into the bottom of 4 pretty dessert glasses. Spoon over a layer of the mascarpone mixture. Add another layer of peaches, then another layer of the mascarpone mixture.

8 Top with a couple of pieces of peach and a sprig of mint. Chill until ready to serve.

Chocolate salami

Who doesn't enjoy a rich, chocolatey, crunchy slice? This is a really quick treat for you to make for afternoon tea or dessert. You just mix everything together and wait for it to set. It doesn't even need to be baked.

You will need

5 oz (150 g) Petit Beurre or Rich Tea cookies (biscuits)

7 oz (200 g) milk or dark chocolate

½ stick (50 g) unsalted butter

plastic bag

rolling pin

plastic wrap (clingfilm)

(makes 8–10 slices)

1 Break the cookies into small pieces—a good way to do this is to put them into a plastic bag, and then lightly crush them with the end of a rolling pin—or alternatively, you can roll the rolling pin over them—until the cookies are broken but not turned into crumbs. Tip them into a mixing bowl.

2 Now melt the chocolate: break it up into pieces and put it in a small heatproof bowl. Ask an adult to help you set the bowl over a saucepan of gently simmering water, making sure that the bottom of the bowl does not touch the water. Stir the chocolate with a wooden spoon until it has melted. Take it off the heat. Alternatively break the chocolate into a microwave-safe bowl. Ask an adult to help you heat it on low for 30 seconds, stir and heat again for another 30 seconds. Keep checking, heating for 30 seconds and stirring until the chocolate is nearly melted (when there are just a few lumps left,) then remove the bowl from the microwave and stir the chocolate until it is smooth Take care that it doesn't overheat.

ROLY-POLY chocolate!

3 Add the butter to the melted chocolate and stir until the butter has melted and mixed in with the chocolate. Leave the mixture to cool for a few minutes.

4 Pour the melted chocolate mixture over the cookies. Make sure you scrape all the chocolate from the sides of the bowl you melted it in. Stir the chocolate and cookies together well.

5 Lay a piece of plastic wrap (clingfilm) on the work surface beside the bowl.

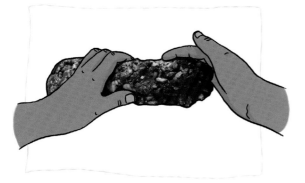

6 Put your clean hands into the bowl and bring all the mixture together into a big lump. Put the lump onto the plastic wrap and make it roughly into a long salami shape about 2 in (5 cm) in diameter (across.) Now you can lick your fingers before washing them well!

7 Roll up the salami tightly in the plastic wrap, trying to pull it into a firm, neat salami shape as you roll. Twist the ends of the wrap together, before you put it into the fridge to set for an hour or so. Cut it into slices to serve.

Ice cream with hot raspberry sauce

I expect you have often eaten ice cream, topped with a squirt of raspberry sauce from a bottle. This is much, much nicer! The hot sauce, made with fresh raspberries, trickles down the side of the ice cream and starts to melt it, making little puddles of creamy raspberry mixture all around the bowl. Irresistible!

You will need

1 lb (450 g) fresh or frozen raspberries (defrosted if frozen)

4–5 tablespoons superfine (caster) sugar

vanilla ice cream

nylon strainer (sieve)

(serves 4)

1 Put the strainer (sieve) over a saucepan and tip in just over half of the raspberries. Squash them with the back of a spoon, pushing them through the strainer so that all the juice is squeezed out into the pan and the seeds (pips) are left behind in the strainer.

2 Add the sugar to the pan and stir it into the juice. Ask an adult to help you heat it gently, over low heat, stirring all the time until the sugar dissolves.

3 Stir in the rest of the whole raspberries.

Real RASPBERRY ripple

4 Place scoops of ice cream into dessert bowls. Carefully pour the hot raspberry sauce over the top and serve immediately.

Chapter 4

Party Food

Roly-poly sandwiches

Smoked salmon is really tasty in these sandwiches and it rolls up easily, but if you don't like fish, you could use thin slices of ham or salami instead. Try different types of bread like whole wheat (wholemeal,) white, or Granary. This is a good recipe to make if you have been growing your own alfalfa sprouts (mustard and cress)——give it a haircut and sprinkle it over the salmon.

You will need

1 slice brown, whole wheat (wholemeal,) white, or Granary bread

1 tablespoon cream cheese

2 slices smoked salmon

alfalfa sprouts (mustard and cress)

rolling pin

(makes 1 sandwich)

 1 Put the slice of bread on a clean surface and use a table knife to cut the crusts off.

2 Flatten the slice of bread by rolling over it with a rolling pin.

Tip: other filling ideas

• Mash a little canned, drained salmon or tuna with a fork and mix in a little mayonnaise. Spread it on the bread then scatter a few torn lettuce or spinach leaves over the top before you roll.

• Grate some cheddar cheese and snip some ham up very small with scissors. Chop a tomato into tiny pieces. Mix everything together and spread on the bread before you roll.

3 Spread the cream cheese onto the bread with the table knife.

4 Lay the smoked salmon on top of the cream cheese and then sprinkle the alfalfa sprouts (mustard and cress) over the salmon.

Super SPIRAL sandwiches

5 Starting with a short side of the bread slice, roll the bread up into a long sausage shape. Using the table knife, cut the sausage shape into five roly-poly sandwiches. When you lay them flat on a plate you'll see that you have made spirals!

roly-poly sandwiches **109**

Green avocado dip with corn chips

Dips are great at parties. This fresh-tasting, bright green one has a Mexican theme as it is made with avocado and has corn chips to scoop it up with. If you and your friends like spicy food, add a few drops of Tabasco sauce at the end to give it some kick!

You will need

4 corn tortillas

1 garlic clove

a handful of fresh cilantro (coriander) leaves

1 lime

2 ripe avocados

a few drops of Tabasco sauce (optional)

baking sheet

a large mortar and pestle or a plastic bowl and a small rolling pin

(serves 4)

1 Ask an adult to heat the oven on to 350°F (180°C) Gas 4. Using scissors, snip the corn tortillas into bite-sized pieces and lay them on a baking sheet. Ask an adult to help you put the sheet into the oven using oven gloves. Bake for 5 minutes until the chips are golden and starting to crisp. Keep checking—they can easily burn! Ask an adult to help you take the chips out of the oven.

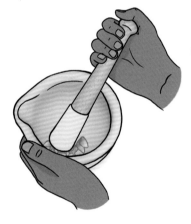

2 Peel the garlic—give it a light bash with a rolling pin first which will make the skin crack and come off easily. If you have a mortar and pestle, put the garlic into the mortar (bowl) and bash with the pestle until you have a paste. If you don't have a mortar and pestle, use the end of a small rolling pin and a plastic bowl.

3 Using scissors, snip the cilantro (coriander) into small pieces and add it to the mortar (or bowl.)

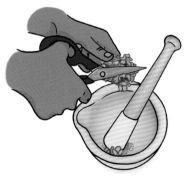

Dip and SCOOP!

4 Cut the lime in half, remembering to use the bridge cutting technique (see page 11.) Squeeze the juice from half of the lime and tip it into the mortar or bowl. Mash everything together with the pestle.

5 Use the bridge cutting technique to cut the avocados in half. Avocados have big pits (stones) in the middle so cut downwards until you reach the pit (stone,) then turn the avocado, cutting as you go, until it is cut through to the pit (stone) all the way around. Twist the two halves and, and they will pull apart.

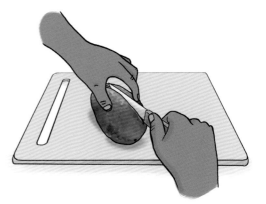

6 Scoop the pits (stones) out of the avocados with a teaspoon and peel away the skins with your fingers. Roughly chop the avocado halves with a table knife.

7 Add some of the avocado flesh to the mortar and mash. Add more avocado flesh and mash again. Keep adding avocado until it has all been added and you have a lumpy paste. If you like your food spicy, add a couple of drops of Tabasco sauce and stir it in. Spoon the dip into a small bowl and serve with the corn chips.

Giant cheese twists

These deliciously crumbly and flaky pastry twists are made even more tasty with a coating of cheese, mustard and a red spice called paprika. They are easy to make as you don't need to do any cutting with sharp knives, and are great finger food for a party.

You will need

13 oz (375 g) package ready-rolled puff pastry

2 tablespoons grainy mustard (or mild mustard)

1 teaspoon mild paprika

1 cup (100 g) grated Parmesan cheese

a little soft butter

2 nonstick baking sheets

a plastic ruler that you have washed and dried

(makes 18 cheese twists)

1 Let the pastry defrost if it is frozen—if not, remove from the fridge about 20 minutes before you want to use it. Sprinkle a little flour on a clean work surface then unwrap and gently unroll and flatten the sheet of pastry. It should measure about 9 x 14½ in (23 x 37 cm.) If your pastry is a different size don't worry, as long as you can cut it into strips about ¾ in (2 cm) wide and about 8 in (20 cm) long it will work. Place it so that the long side is at the top of the work surface.

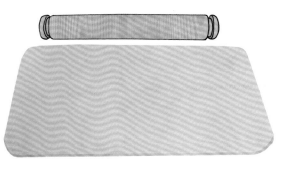

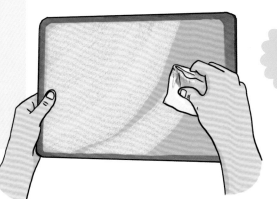

2 Rub the baking sheets with a little soft butter on a kitchen towel to grease them. This will stop the twists sticking to the sheet.

3 Mix the mustard with the paprika. Dot teaspoons of this mixture all over the pastry and then use a table knife to spread it out evenly, going right to the edges.

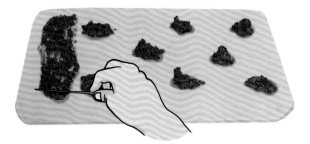

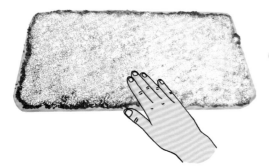

4 If you need to grate the cheese, use a fine cheese grater to grate it onto a plate. Use your fingers to sprinkle the cheese in an even layer over the top of the mustard mix, then gently press the cheese onto the pastry with your fingertips or the back of a spoon.

5 Cut the pastry into 18 even strips about ¾ in (2 cm) wide, cutting from top to bottom with a table knife. A well-washed plastic ruler might help you keep the lines straight!

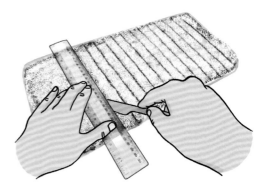

6 Take one strip and hold an end in each hand. Keep one hand still and turn the other to make a twist in the strip. Keep twisting until it is twisted all along its length. Then put it down onto the work surface and gently roll it with your hands, as if making a sausage from play dough, so the twist picks up any cheese that has dropped off, and it is tightly twisted. Put the twist on the prepared baking sheet, and make the rest in the same way.

7 Put the sheets of twists in the fridge for about 15 minutes. Meanwhile, ask an adult to preheat the oven to 400° F (200°C) Gas 6. When it is hot, put on oven gloves and ask an adult to help you take the sheets out of the fridge and put them into the oven. Bake for 15 minutes or until the twists are brown and crispy.

Spicy, twisty, cheesy, and crunchy!

8 Ask an adult to help you remove the baking sheets from the oven. Leave the twists to cool on the sheets for 5 minutes, then carefully lift them onto a wire rack using a metal spatula. Leave to cool completely. Eat as soon as possible or store in an airtight container for up to 2 days.

Sausage rolls

No party is complete without a heaped dish of hot, bite-sized sausage rolls. All you need to add is a bowl of ketchup to dip them in.

You will need

....

13 oz (375 g) ready-rolled puff pastry

1 tablespoon Dijon mustard

24 cocktail sausages

1 egg

a baking sheet

nonstick baking parchment

scissors

pencil

(makes 24)

1 Put the baking sheet on top of the nonstick baking parchment and draw around it with a pencil. Cut out around the pencil lines and put the paper on top of the baking sheet—this is called lining and will stop the sausage rolls from sticking to the baking sheet.

2 Let the pastry defrost if it is frozen—if not, remove it from the fridge about 20 minutes before you want to use it. Sprinkle a little flour on a clean work surface, then unwrap and gently unroll and flatten the sheet of pastry. Unroll it so the long side is at the top of the work surface.

3 Use a table knife to spread the mustard thinly over the pastry.

4 Cut pastry vertically into six strips all roughly the same width. Cut each strip in half and then in half again so there are four pieces for each strip.

Place a sausage on each piece of pastry and roll the pastry around it pressing the ends together where they overlap. Arrange them on the lined baking tray.

Sausages with COATS on!

6 Carefully use a small sharp knife to make two or three small cuts in the top of each sausage roll.

7 Break the egg into a small bowl. To do this tap it firmly on the side of the bowl to crack it. (Not too hard or you will smash it completely!) Then put your thumbs into the crack and pull the two halves apart. Pick out any pieces of shell with a bigger piece of shell. Beat it with a fork to mix it all together. Then use a pastry brush to brush beaten egg all over the top of the sausage rolls.

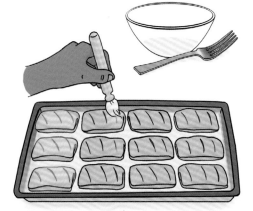

8 Ask an adult to preheat the oven to 375°F (190°C) Gas 5. When it is hot, put on oven gloves and ask an adult to help you put the baking sheet on the middle shelf of the preheated oven. Bake for 30 minutes, or until golden. Ask an adult to help you remove the sheet from the oven, let them cool for a few minutes then carefully lift the sausage rolls onto a serving plate using a metal spatula.

Chicken drumsticks

Play at being cavemen at your party and get everyone gnawing on chicken drumsticks. You can cook them the day before a party(or a picnic or even a school day—they are great in a lunch box) and then keep them in the fridge overnight.

You will need

1 onion

1 garlic clove

8 tablespoons tomato ketchup

2 tablespoons soft dark brown sugar

1 tablespoon wholegrain mustard

1 tablespoon Worcestershire sauce

8 chicken drumsticks

garlic press

a heavy-based ovenproof dish

(serves 8)

1 Peel the papery outside skin off the onion and put it on a chopping board. Using the bridge technique (see page 11,) cut the onion in half with a sharp knife. Be very careful—onions are slippery and the knife can easily slip off. Lay each half flat on the board, trim off any hairy roots and now, with your hand in the claw position, cut each half into very small pieces. Put the onion pieces into a large bowl.

2 Peel the garlic—give it a light bash with a rolling pin first which will make the skin crack and come off easily, then put it into a garlic press and squeeze it into the bowl with the onion. Add the tomato ketchup, sugar, mustard, and Worcestershire sauce and stir everything together.

3 Using a small, sharp knife, score two or three cuts into each piece of chicken.

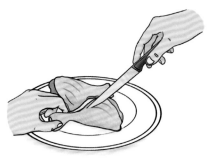

GNAW it like a caveman!

4 Add the chicken to the bowl and use your clean hands to cover it with the marinade, spreading it over the chicken skin, especially where the cuts are. Now, WASH YOUR HANDS—you must always wash your hands with plenty of soap and hot water after handling raw meat, especially chicken.

5 Cover the bowl with plastic wrap (clingfilm) and put it in the fridge for 15–30 minutes. This will allow all the lovely flavors to soak into the chicken. Meanwhile, ask an adult to preheat the oven to 400°F (200°C) Gas 6.

6 Arrange the chicken drumsticks in a heavy-based ovenproof dish. Put on oven gloves and ask an adult to help you put it in the oven to roast for 40–45 minutes. Two or three times during the cooking, put on oven gloves and ask an adult to help you take the chicken out of the oven. Use tongs to turn it over before putting it back. That way it will get brown all over.

7 When it is ready, take the dish out of the oven and leave it to cool. You could eat it immediately, when warm, or put it in the fridge overnight, ready for the party the next day.

Chocolate-dipped strawberries

Nearly everyone loves strawberries and nearly everyone loves chocolate, so what better party snack can there be than these chocolate-dipped strawberries? They are also easy to make, easy to eat and look really pretty on your party table!

You will need

1 large bar of good-quality chocolate (milk, dark, or white)

a few handfuls of ripe strawberries with the hulls (green stalks) still on

(makes lots!)

1 First melt the chocolate. You can do this in two ways, but for both ways, it is very important that you do not overheat the chocolate or it will spoil.

To melt it on the stovetop (hob): find a small heatproof bowl that will sit on top of a saucepan, so that the bottom of the bowl is just under the rim of the pan. Break up the chocolate and put it in the bowl. Ask an adult to help you set the bowl over the saucepan of gently simmering water, making sure that the bottom of the bowl does not touch the water. Stir the chocolate with a wooden spoon until it has almost all melted with just a few lumps left. Take it off the heat and stir it until it until it is smooth.

To melt it in a microwave: break the chocolate into a microwave-safe bowl. Ask an adult to help you heat it on low for 30 seconds, then stir it and then heat it again for another 30 seconds. Keep checking, heating for 30 seconds and stirring until the chocolate is nearly melted with just a few lumps left. Remove the bowl from the microwave and stir it until it is smooth.

Tip:

It is really important that the strawberries are dry—do not let any water drip into the chocolate because even a tiny amount can cause the chocolate to become hard and turn into a solid lump! If you have washed your strawberries, leave them on paper towels (kitchen paper) until they are completely dry.

2

Hold a strawberry by its stalk and dip just the bottom half of it into the chocolate. Hold it over the bowl for a few seconds to let any chocolate drip off, and then put it on a plate and leave it to set. Keep going until all the chocolate or all the strawberries have been used up.

Chocolate **AND** strawberries —what could be better?

Marshmallow pops

This is your chance to buy a selection of all the pretty sprinkles that you can buy in supermarkets these days! Making these pops is a great party activity to do with your friends. Ask an adult to melt the three types of chocolate at the same time and then you can all get around a table to have a go!

You will need

5 oz (150 g) dark chocolate

5 oz (150 g) milk chocolate

5 oz (150 g) white chocolate

7 oz (200 g) large marshmallows

edible sprinkles, finely chopped nuts and/or dried (desiccated) coconut

nonstick parchment paper

about 20–25 wooden popsicle (lolly) sticks

(makes 20–25)

1 Cut two sheets of parchment paper—one to put your finished pops on, and one to catch any sprinkles which fall off the pops as you work. (Have a sheet for each person if you are doing this with friends.) Pour your sprinkles, nuts, and coconut into small bowls so they are easy to get to.

2 Choose which type of chocolate you want to start with—work with one type at a time unless you have friends helping you make them. Melt the chocolate. You can do this in two ways but for both ways it is very important that you do not overheat the chocolate or it will spoil.

To melt it on the stovetop (hob): find a small heatproof bowl that will sit on top of a saucepan, so that the bottom of the bowl is just under the rim of the pan. Break up the chocolate and put it in the bowl. Ask an adult to help you set the bowl over the saucepan of gently simmering water, making sure that the bottom of the bowl does not touch the water. Stir the chocolate with a wooden spoon until it has almost all melted with just a few lumps left. Take it off the heat and stir it until it until it is smooth.

To melt it in a microwave: break the chocolate into a microwave-safe bowl. Ask an adult to help you heat it on low for 30 seconds, then stir it and heat it again for another 30 seconds. Keep checking, heating for 30 seconds and stirring until the chocolate is nearly melted with just a few lumps left. Remove the bowl from the microwave and stir it until it is smooth.

3

Push a popsicle (lolly) stick through two marshmallows.

Why not make pops at your PARTY?

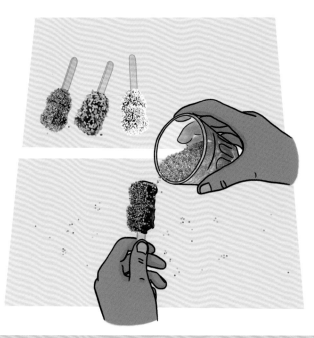

4

Dip the marshmallows into the melted chocolate so that they are completely coated in chocolate. Use a spoon to help you finish coating the marshmallows. If there is too much chocolate let it drip back into the bowl.

5

Working over one sheet of parchment paper, sprinkle the chocolate-coated marshmallows with the sprinkles, chopped nuts and/or desiccated coconut, then lay it down and leave it to set on the other sheet of parchment. (You can use the paper you are working over to tip any sprinkles that fall off back into the bowl.) Make as many marshmallow pops as you can with this type of chocolate then wash up the bowl and start on the next.

Sweet popcorn

Everyone should have a go at making their own popcorn. It is like magic—noisy magic—when the small hard corn kernels explode into the big fluffy popcorn pieces we all love to eat. This recipe uses a little sugar to sweeten the corn, but there is a list of other flavors you could try. Although it is a very easy recipe, it is a Level 3 because you need to handle a very hot pan—an adult should do this.

You will need

2 tablespoons sunflower oil

⅓ cup (65 g) popping corn

1 tablespoon golden superfine (caster) sugar (optional)

a large saucepan with a lid (a glass lid lets you see the corn popping)

(serves 2–3)

Tip: other good things to add to popcorn

• Mix a pinch of cinnamon into the sugar or use vanilla sugar instead of ordinary sugar.
• Soft light brown sugar gives a more toffee-like flavor.
• For stickier popcorn stir in one tablespoon of corn (golden) syrup or maple syrup.
• For savory popcorn, add a little salt or try adding 2 oz (50 g) finely grated Cheddar or Parmesan cheese.

1 Put the oil into a large saucepan and ask an adult to heat it until it is hot.

2 Tip the corn kernels into the pan, and shake the pan gently so that the corn covers the whole of the saucepan base.

3 Cook the corn until it starts to pop, then put the lid on immediately. If you have a pan with a glass lid, you will be able to watch it pop.

Pop... pop... pop... POP!

4 Cook the corn for 2–3 more minutes. Hold the lid on tightly and shake it often. Listen and keep cooking until the sound of popping stops.

5 Remove from the heat, take off the lid and tip into a serving bowl. Add the sugar and stir gently with a wooden spoon.

Suppliers

You will probably already have most of the equipment needed for these recipes in your kitchen, but for additional cookware supplies and, in particular, child-friendly equipment, try the following stores.

US Suppliers

Fancy Flours Inc
www.fancyflours.com

Growing Cooks
www.growingcooks.com

Local Cooking Classes
www.localcookingclasses.com

Michaels
www.michaels.com

Sugarcrafts
www.sugarcrafts.com

Williams-Sonoma
www.williams-sonoma.com

Wilton
www.wilton.com

UK Suppliers

Cookify
www.cookify.co.uk

Hobbycraft
www.hobbycraft.co.uk

John Lewis
www.johnlewis.com

Lakeland
www.lakeland.co.uk

Spotty Green Frog
www.spottygreenfrog.co.uk

Squires Kitchen
www.squires-shop.com

Sugar Shack
www.sugarshack.co.uk

Index

Acknowledgments

Key: l = left, r = right, t = top, b = bottom, c=center

RECIPES

Annie Rigg: 18, 24, 92, 116, 122; Amanda Grant: 22, 28, 31, 37, 40, 44, 58, 64, 74, 84, 90, 108, 110, 118, 120, 124; Liz Franklin: 34, 68, 76, 80, 96, 100, 104; Linda Collister: 46, 50, 54, 62, 72, 88

PHOTOGRAPHY

Tara Fisher: 1, 29, 13, 33, 37, 39, 41, 43, 45, 48, 65, 67, 75, 119, 121, 125; Lisa Linder: 2, 6, 9, 19, 21, 27, 35, 69, 71, 77, 81, 83, 93, 94, 97, 101, 103, 105, 106, 117, 123; Susan Bell: 3, 5c, 15, 16, 23, 59, 84, 85, 91, 109, 111, 112; Vanessa Davies: 5t, 5c, 14, 47, 51, 55, 63, 73, 89; Polly Wreford: 5b, 115

STYLING

Amanda Grant: 1, 3, 5c, 16, 23, 33, 37, 39, 41, 43, 45, 48, 59, 75, 84, 85, 91, 109, 111, 112, 121; Joy Skipper: 2, 9, 35, 81, 83, 97, 105; Helen Trent: 5t, 5c, 14, 47, 51, 55, 63, 73, 89, 115; Liz Belton: 6, 93, 94, 106, 117, 119, 123, 125

COVER PHOTOGRAPHY

Back cover tc/tr: Lisa Linder; back cover cl: Susan Bell; back cover c: Polly Wreford; back cover cr: Tara Fisher; back cover br: Vanessa Davies; spine: Lisa Linder; front cover cl: Tara Fisher; front cover tr: Susan Bell; front cover cr/br: Lisa Linder